Y0-FKV-887

The Essential Edgar Allan Poe

William Pack

The Essential Edgar Allan Poe
Copyright © 2014 by William Pack

All rights reserved. No part of this book may be reproduced or transmitted in any form or by any means without written permission from the author.

williampack.com

ISBN 13: 978-1512387117
ISBN 10: 1512387118

Printed in USA

R07116 95425

For Elaine

Table of Contents

Acknowledgements

First, I wish to remind you that this book is the product of secondary sources. Peter Ackroyd, James Hutchisson, Jeffrey Meyers, Kenneth Silverman, Daniel Stashower, and John Evangelist Walsh all wrote excellent books on Poe. Those books and others are the basis for my work and are listed in the bibliography.

I hope my book will lead you to read one or more of those more detailed works.

As always, my work is the product of the chances that come my way. Mary Ann Lema, librarian from the Prairie Trails Library in Burbank, Illinois, originally suggested Poe as a possible program. I owe her a big thank you for starting this journey.

I need to thank Kevin Moriarty and Brandon Fink for their eagle-eyed editing skills.

Of all that I have, I am most thankful for Elaine Cassell. She makes everything I do better. Her support, advice, and editing have been invaluable. Sometimes it takes me a while, but eventually I agree with all her suggestions. I look forward to the future chapters we'll write together.

Any mistakes in this manuscript are entirely the fault of a stubborn author.

Thank you for supporting books printed on actual paper!

Edgar Allan Poe 1847 (Library of Congress)

Introduction

"I knew something of Poe, something of the unfathomed gulfs of darkness out of which the lightning of his genius sent its scorching flashes." —Walter Colton

I discovered Edgar Allan Poe like most people, through the movies. In the 1960s, American International Pictures produced a popular series of Technicolor films based on Poe's works. Directed by Roger Corman and starring Vincent Price, they were the "Hollywood" version of his stories, part Poe, part schlock, part comedy. In the glow of the TV, late at night, with the Son of Svengoolie as my host, they were scary, *but not that scary.* In knowing those movies, I thought I knew what Poe stories were all about. I made a bad mistake, but many of his earliest biographers made a worse one, confusing the writing for the man.

He has been seen variously as the original "goth" or "emo" who always wore black and lived in a state of melancholy, a raving lunatic, a drug addict, a drunkard, or a twisted and evil man. For his personality and his writing, he has been equally praised and vilified.

The facts of his life are far more complicated and human. He was a man both blessed and cursed by genius. I hope I have captured the fullness of Poe in a concise and enlightening way. The Edgar Allan Poe you will meet here was a true southern gentleman, a remarkable athlete, and a soldier. He was also a dark and disturbed figure, an oversensitive artist, an intermittent binge drinker, a man scarred by unrelenting emotional trauma. He perceived his own genius and still possessed insecurities. Overcompensating with an oversized ego, he didn't suffer fools and felt most people were fools. He alienated almost every friend he ever had. The son of actors, he once wrote in a letter that, "The world shall be my theatre" and he lived life with a conscious theatrical flourish. He was famous (and infamous) in his time.

Through his work, he was a central figure in the building of American literature. His writing is modern, so much so that I always *imagined* him living in the 1890s or early 1900s, but nothing was further from the truth.

For someone whose death came early, his influence on the literary world was long-lived. Edgar virtually invented three literary genres: horror, detective, and science fiction. Writers from Robert Louis Stevenson to Rudyard Kipling, from Oscar Wilde to F. Scott Fitzgerald, borrowed themes and literary techniques from Poe. His notoriously harsh critiques taught the nation the role of a literary critic. He set the "rules" for a new form of fiction writing called the short story. He revolutionized poetry from a common recounting of an event to the depiction of a psychological state. He even puzzled his readers with a popular cryptography magazine column. The sheer variety and quality of his articles and stories is staggering. It would take decades for his audience to catch up to his writing.

Perhaps you thought he was just a ghoul that went bump in the night?

The true revelation is that his work is deeply autobiographical.

Edgar distorted and exaggerated, but the themes, the people, all drawn from his real world. He returned to them again and again. He worked out his torments and even engaged in fantasies of revenge against those he thought wronged him.

If you think you know Poe from the movies or think you know his stories from the same, I will not delay you any further. Not only do you hold his story in your hands, but also I've included a small selection of his poetry and a few of his most accessible stories. If you haven't read either, you will discover Poe full of surprises.

The Raven (Edmund Dulac 1912)

Act One
1809 - 1826
Childhood

Edgar's mother Eliza Poe (Library of Congress)

"From childhood's hour I have not been
As others were—I have not seen
As others saw—I could not bring
My passions from a common spring—
From the same source I have not taken
My sorrow—I could not awaken
My heart to joy at the same tone—
And all I lov'd—I lov'd alone."

Edgar held his inheritance in his delicate hands, a small watercolor sketch of Boston Harbor that his mother, Eliza, painted a year before his birth. Just short of being three years old, he was too young to grasp the full meaning of her death. What few memories he later had were manufactured by his creative mind and from the stories of those who knew her. His grief and loss would become more oppressive as the years passed. He searched, but never filled the void she left. Her death haunted his writing. He said, "The death of a beautiful woman is, unquestionably, the most poetical topic in the world," and he returned to the subject often.

Eliza was the daughter of Elizabeth Arnold, a British actress. Elizabeth's husband and Eliza's father passed when she was two years old. Later, in 1796, Mother and daughter emigrated to America. At the age of nine, she made her stage debut to rave reviews. Together, they toured with a troupe of actors for two years, until her mother contracted yellow fever and died. At eleven years old Eliza was without family, on her own.

The manager of their performing troupe took responsibility for Eliza and she continued to work on the stage. Her mother had instilled in her a professional discipline for stagecraft and by her mid-teens, Eliza knew about seventy parts from Shakespeare to light comedy. Critics praised her as being one of the most promising actors on the American stage. They also remarked on her beauty, her large doe eyes, raven-black hair, and slight figure.

At fifteen, she married seventeen year old actor, Charles Hopkins. They played the Virginia stage circuit for three years, until Charles fell ill (probably yellow fever) and died. Eliza, now eighteen, was a widow. She still had her work, and in Richmond she met a twenty-one year old actor that would become her second husband.

Baltimore-born David Poe Jr. was the son of a locally celebrated Revolutionary War hero. Against his family's wishes, he rejected the study of law to become an actor. His good looks and deep voice seemed to bode well for success, but none was forthcoming. He lacked talent for the stage and it became more pronounced in contrast to Eliza's growing accomplishments. Nevertheless, they married six months after the death of her first husband on March 14, 1806.

Within a year Eliza gave birth to her first child. William Henry Poe was born on January 30, 1807, in Boston. A struggling actor's life was no place for a child, so they temporarily shipped him off to live with his paternal grandparents.

The birth of Edgar on January 19, 1809 strained their finances and relationship further. There were no relatives to take care of him.

Reputedly, David never refused a glass of ale or a fistfight. He missed several performances due to drunkenness. Faced with withering criticism on the performances he did make, he threatened to beat up several critics. Sometime between the fall of 1809 and the summer of 1810, David abandoned his family. (Nothing is known about him after this time, although some sources report he died in Norfolk, alone, on or about December 11, 1811. Both he and Eliza had shown signs of tuberculosis even before the birth of Edgar.)

On her own at twenty-two, Eliza continued to work and care for her children. Her success on stage did not translate to making a living. Often benefit performances were put on to provide relief of her "private misfortunes." The proceeds of the ticket sales going directly to her.

She needed aid more than ever, for she was pregnant again. The uncertain lapse of time between David Poe's disappearance and the third child's birth stirred rumors that the child was illegitimate. In December 1810 came a daughter, Rosalie.

The desertion of her husband, the arduous demands of work, the constant travel and the sole responsibility of her children undoubtedly hastened her early death. She made her last stage appearance in October 1811. She ended up back in Richmond—bedridden, a charity case.

The women of Richmond society took up Eliza as one of their "causes." On November 29, the Richmond Theater, encouraged by the women, announced a benefit for Eliza. The *Richmond Enquirer* reported her hopeless condition and asked for help: "On this night, *Mrs. Poe*, lingering on the bed of disease and surrounded by her children, asks your assistance; and *asks it perhaps for the last time*."

Nine days later, December 8, 1811 she died. She was twenty-four.

In her brief life, she had been orphaned, married, widowed, married again, abandoned, given birth to three children, and performed on stage more than three hundred times.

Eliza's three children remained with her during her illness. Fellow actors and friends, Harriet and Luke Usher, took care of them. Her son, William Henry, at the time five years old, later recalled that she spoke a long last farewell to them. She had little to leave them. Edgar, who bore a striking resemblance to her, received a miniature portrait of Eliza, some letters, and her watercolor sketch of Boston Harbor. On the back of it, she wrote, "For my little son Edgar, who should ever love Boston, the place of his birth, and where his mother found her *best,* and *most sympathetic* friends."

Edgar did not respect her request. In adult life, he nourished a strong dislike for the city of his birth. The loss of his parents and the estrangement from the place of his birth left him a perpetual orphan. In a letter written years later, Edgar said of his mother, "I myself never knew her—and never knew the affection of a father. Both died…within weeks of each other. I have many occasional dealings with Adversity, but the want of parental affection has been the heaviest of my trials."

One of the Richmond society women, which took care of Eliza, was Frances "Fanny" Allan. She took an immediate liking to Edgar, and he to her. She resembled his mother: slight figure, large dark eyes, and girlish. Twenty-six years old and childless, she loved Edgar as her own. She too had been an orphan and convinced her husband to bring the boy into their home.

At first, the tough Scotsman, John Allan, objected, but even though he was a focused man of business, he had a reputation for generosity. He had a strong streak of self-reliance. Also an orphan, Allan had been raised by a strict, no nonsense uncle. His uncle denied him the full care and generosity he felt he deserved. Allan prided himself in being a self-made, self-educated man who despised dependence. Yet, he tried to give the dependent Edgar the liberal education he missed. As the years passed, Edgar grew into the type of person John Allan disliked—emotional, flighty, unreliable, and preoccupied with pursuits that had no material or financial value, like poetry and art.

One of the greatest difficulties for Edgar was that the Allans never formally adopted him. This left him with a permanent unease due to the lack of a stable family. He was christened, in January of 1812, with the name Edgar Allan Poe. (Once Edgar left the Allans, he rarely used their surname, signing himself "Edgar A. Poe" or "E.A. Poe" and occasionally "Edgar Poe.")

Few scraps of information survive describing Edgar's early years in the Allan house. Mostly it appears to be a normal childhood for the time and circumstances. Edgar found himself in a world very different from the one he left. John Allan was a successful and affluent merchant and Fanny lavished affection on, if not spoiled, the boy. Edgar was described as "a lovely little fellow, with dark curls and brilliant eyes...charming every one by his childish grace, vivacity, and cleverness." He displayed a retentive memory, learning and reciting beautiful passages of English poetry.

He continued to keep in contact with his siblings by writing his brother, who went back to his paternal grandparents, and visiting his sister who was adopted by a family that lived nearby.

In the late spring of 1815, business was good enough that John Allan and his partners decided to open an office in England. Fanny fought the move. She hated the thought of leaving Richmond, but John assured her the trip would be short, no more than a couple of years.

After a brief visit with his relatives in Scotland, John Allan moved the family to London and dedicated himself to his business. Doing business in a new country where he was a stranger meant making new alliances and learning a new set of customs and practices. John Allan was clever, persistent, and patient. After a slow start and two years of diligent work, the business prospered.

Edgar was sent off to two different boarding schools. He appeared to flourish in his schoolwork. He studied Latin, French, and other classical subjects, even taking dance lessons. Yet, he chafed under the yoke of English education. It emphasized mechanical rote memorization, often cruelly administered, and without any attempt to make it relevant to Edgar's inquisitive mind.

The master of his second school, Reverend John Bansby, said, "Edgar Allan was a quick and clever boy and would have been a very good boy if he had had not been spoilt by his parents, but they spoilt him, and allowed him an extravagant amount of pocket-money, which enabled him to get into all manner of mischief—still I like the boy—poor fellow, his parents spoilt him!" On another occasion he said, "Allan was intelligent, wayward, and willful."

While he seemed to succeed as a scholar, he hid his despair. Years later, Edgar would say that his time at the schools was lonely and unhappy. The time away from his caretakers, with unfamiliar people, in a strange country, angered and frightened him. It only increased his unease, feelings of abandonment, and lack of belonging.

His visits back home did not set his mind at ease. John Allan was a prisoner of London and his business. Fanny, prone to illnesses (both real and imagined), was often shut up in a dark room away from the family and unavailable to Edgar. Her husband was impatient with his wife's many upsets. He bluntly stated that she was "never without complaint." John Allan had a lust for the pleasures of life; he drank and ate well, and carried on several affairs. He fathered at least two illegitimate children back in Richmond.

Edgar was virtually alone.

With little warning, after three and a half years abroad, the London tobacco market collapsed. It broke business after business until the chain reached John Allan. He was bankrupt. He arranged to pay off his creditors and, with their consent, he returned to Richmond where he could put his affairs back in order.

On July 21, 1820, after a voyage of thirty-six days, John Allan and his family arrived in New York. He wrote a friend that Fanny had been intensely seasick during the rough voyage and complained about the extreme heat on their arrival in New York. She felt so unwell he sent for a doctor.

Unsettled and financially troubled, the Allans moved several times, living with business partners and relatives in Richmond. Despite the hardships, Edgar continued his schooling.

The schools of the time were not part of a public system. They were private academies of about 20 students. The course of study focused on the classics: Greek, Latin, French, English composition, mathematics, and some science.

As Edgar grew, he read Cicero, Virgil, Horace, and Ovid in Latin, as well as, Homer in Greek. His teacher at the time, Joseph Clarke, gave a favorable estimate of the generous character, enthusiastic ardor, intellectual capacity, and poetic power of his talented pupil: "His natural and predominate passion seemed to be an enthusiastic ardor in everything he undertook; in his difference of opinion with his fellow students, he was tenacious, and would not yield till his judgment was convinced. As a scholar, he was ambitious to excel, and tho' not conspicuously studious, always acquitted himself well in his classes. His imaginative powers seemed to take precedence of all his other facilities; he gave proof of this, in some juvenile compositions addressed to his young female friends. He had a sensitive and tender heart, and would strain every nerve to oblige a friend."

Edgar was adept at scanning poetry and in "capping verses"—an exercise in which one student would quote a line of Latin verse and the other had to quote another line beginning with the same letter. He committed hundreds of lines of English verse to memory, and tried his hand at writing some of his own. Clarke called Edgar a born artist, who wrote genuine poetry while other boys manufactured mechanical verse.

When he was eleven years old, Edgar wanted John Allan to

publish a manuscript of his poems. Clarke advised Allan against the project, thinking this would worsen Edgar's inordinate vanity.

At fourteen, Edgar entered William Burke's school where he continued his studies. It is rather surprising, in view of the popular image of Poe, to find young Edgar a skillful athlete who liked to roam the countryside on daring adventures. He was strong, wiry, and highly competitive. He was a swift runner, a trained boxer, and avid sportsman. A classmate recalled him being "the best, the most daring, and most enduring swimmer that I ever saw in the water."

Around fifteen or sixteen, he became locally famous for swimming six miles in the James River under a hot June sun and against a strong tide. Edgar undertook the challenge as a wager and walked home afterward seemingly unaffected by the strenuous stunt.

For all his positives, Edgar's sociability stopped at the school house doors. He never asked any of his mates to come home after class. His childhood tragedy, low social status, and artistic temperament made him feel like, and actually be, an exceptional, isolated individual.

Colonel James Preston, a classmate, said, "He was self-willed, capricious, inclined to be imperious, and though of generous impulses, not steadily kind or even amiable. . .Of Edgar Poe it was known that his parents were players [actors] and that he was dependent upon the bounty that is bestowed upon an adopted son. All this had the effect of making the boys decline his leadership; and on looking back on it since, I fancy it gave him a fierceness he would otherwise not have had."

He treated sickly Fanny Allan as his mother, but it could only be at a distance. Edgar's need for female sympathy and protection led him to seek mother figures elsewhere. He courted several young girls including his neighbor Elmira Royster. Edgar was serious enough to propose marriage, but interference from her father ended any hope of consummating the relationship. Edgar would never forget her.

He developed an infatuation with a friend's mother, Jane Stanard. He gave her all the affectionate devotion of a son. Throughout his life, Edgar would have an unerring ability to be drawn to tragic women who were much like his birth mother. Jane resembled Eliza and Fanny, in both appearance and temperament.

She was frequently ill and fell into a long period of depression. Eventually, she went insane and died about a year later, April 1824, in an asylum, possibly of "brain cancer."

Edgar visited her grave often, and he told a female admirer that he shed tears in the freshly dug earth.

The upset of the loss triggered a prolonged episode of depression in Edgar. He was miserable, "sulky," and "ill-tempered." John Allan interpreted this mood as a sign of thanklessness. Allan resented Edgar's increasing maturity and independence. Edgar seemingly refused or was unable to express his gratitude.

To make matters worse, John Allan was still laboring under the large debt he owed from the failure of his business. He couldn't understand this perceived transformation from darling child to ungrateful son. As a further insult, John Allan wrote Edgar's brother a bitter self-righteous letter complaining about the boy.

John Allan's and Edgar's mutual resentments, the gap between this precocious, brilliant poet and the self-made, rough and ready tobacco merchant ultimately will lay the groundwork for a lasting estrangement.

Suddenly, in a remarkable reversal of misfortune, the Allans' pressing financial problems were solved when John Allan's uncle, William Galt, suddenly died in 1825. John Allan received an inheritance of more than $750,000—a fortune.

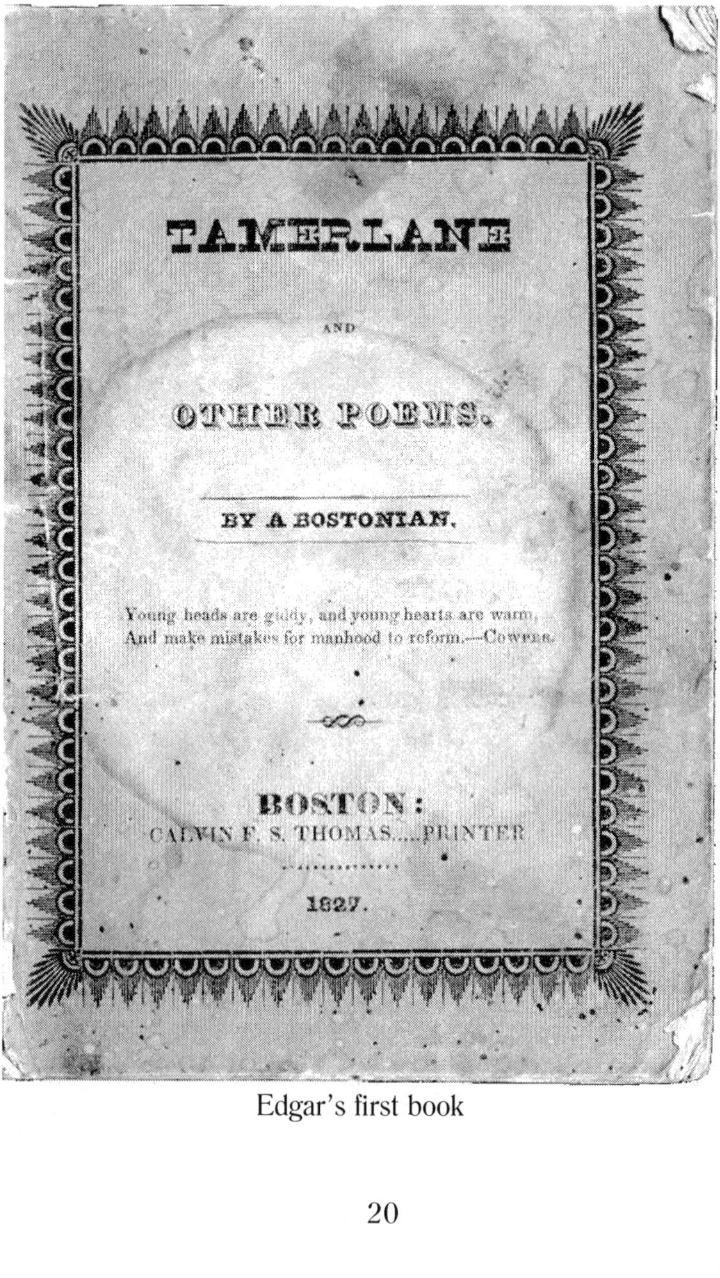

Edgar's first book

Act Two
1826 - 1831
Independence

AN EARLY POEM BY EDGAR ALLAN POE.

THE following verses, which are given in fac-simile, were written by Edgar A. Poe, shortly after he left West Point in 1829. Poe was then only 19 years old. The fact that these verses were written in the album of a lady of distinguished social position is alone sufficient to contradict the statement of Griswold, that, after leaving West Point, Poe was a homeless and friendless wanderer. He had found a home with his aunt and adopted mother, Mrs. Clemm, who was his first, last, and best friend.

E. L. D.

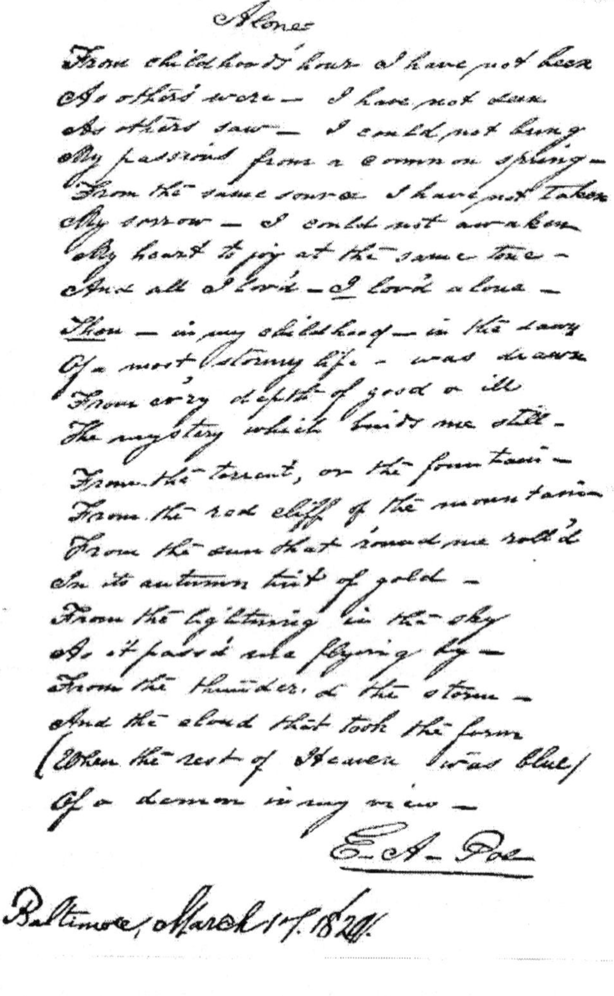
Alone

From childhood's hour I have not been
As others were — I have not seen
As others saw — I could not bring
My passions from a common spring —
From the same source I have not taken
My sorrow — I could not awaken
My heart to joy at the same tone —
And all I lov'd — I lov'd alone —
Then — in my childhood — in the dawn
Of a most stormy life — was drawn
From ev'ry depth of good or ill
The mystery which binds me still —
From the torrent, or the fountain —
From the red cliff of the mountain —
From the sun that 'round me roll'd
In its autumn tint of gold —
From the lightning in the sky
As it pass'd me flying by —
From the thunder, & the storm —
And the cloud that took the form
(When the rest of Heaven was blue)
Of a demon in my view —

E. A. Poe

Baltimore, March 17. 1829.

"I have thrown myself on the world,
like the Norman Conqueror
on the shores of Britain
and by my avowed assurance of victory,
have destroyed the fleet which could alone
cover my retreat—
I must either conquer or die—
succeed or be disgraced."

Late February 1826, Edgar left Richmond for Charlottesville to enroll in Thomas Jefferson's year old University of Virginia. The university was unlike any other. Jefferson envisioned an "academical village" in which students set their own course of study. He established a system of minimal rules and maximum self-governance.

His system failed.

Student life was chaotic, even dangerous. During a riot in the school's first year, masked students threw bricks and bottles at professors. Not only the students, but also even the professors ignored the rules, at least one horsewhipped his wife in the street.. Tobacco, wine, liquor, servants, horses, dogs, and guns were strictly forbidden and frequently enjoyed. Gambling and dueling were both prohibited, yet commonplace.

Despite the chaos and being three years younger than his average classmate, Edgar excelled in his studies. He delighted in his natural scholarly instincts. He enrolled in courses in ancient and modern languages. He also joined the Jefferson Society, a debating club, and became known for his verbal facility. One classmate said that Edgar rarely had to prepare his lessons in advance and only studied a few minutes before class in order to give the best recitation in the group.

For all his success in the academic world, he failed in the social one. Classmates reported that Edgar's behavior was wild and erratic. At times, he was frolicsome, full of fun, and entertained with poetry, "then suddenly a change would come over him." Upon the walls of his dormitory, he would draw "whimsical, fanciful, and grotesque figures with so much artistic skill." Fellow students debated if Edgar would become a great artist or great writer. Many recalled that he was gloomy, morose, standoffish, and touchy. He seemed to have a chip on his shoulder. "He was very excitable and restless, at times wayward, and melancholic."

Edgar desperately desired closeness, but so feared it or the loss of it, that he sabotaged his chances at it.

He had a great talent and an appetite for work, but needed an external structure. Years later, he blamed his alcoholism on his time at the university. Charles Baudelaire attributed Edgar's drinking to his suicidal impulses: "he did not drink like an ordinary toper, but like a savage…as though he was accomplishing an act of murder, as though there was something inside him that he had to kill." He drank and gambled in a joyless, but impassioned manner that amounted to a frenzy. Being competitive, emotional, and feeling superior to…well…everyone, Edgar played cards badly and lost. He owed more than $2,000 in gambling debts.

As Edgar's financial problems increased, the conflicts with John Allan escalated. He blamed Allan for forcing him to gamble, for failing to provide enough money to pay his university expenses. Allegations flew back and forth, charges real and unfounded. To the rock-hard parsimonious Allan, Edgar seemed to be living the life of a wastrel.

In fairness, it seems Allan deliberately sent Edgar to school with insufficient funds, placing him in an impossible situation. It is curious that Allan provided an expensive English education while business was bad and he had no money, but was unwilling to do the same now that he had a fortune. For whatever reason, it reflects a radical change in how he would treat his charge.

In December 1826, Allan retrieved the 17 year old Edgar from school. Allan refused to finance any further period of study and condemned him to work at his Richmond business without pay, doing accounting, bookkeeping, and correspondence.

By March of 1827, Edgar ran off. He ended up in Boston working various odd jobs with little success. With no money or prospects, he enlisted as Edgar A. Perry into the army. There was no reason to lie, except to disappear.

The army would alleviate his poverty, offer security and provide the necessities of life. Edgar also craved the certainty of army life, the structure, discipline, and paternal authority.

At this time, Edgar somehow published his first book, a forty-page volume entitled, *Tamerlane and Other Poems.* Heavily influenced by the poems of Lord Byron, (the most fashionable poet of the day) the autobiographical work has a strong sense of form, cadence, and meter; with a mood of mournfulness and introspection. Fifty copies were printed and only twelve copies are known to exist, making it one of the rarest and most valuable American first editions. In a most curious act of self-sabotage, he released it anonymously as "A Bostonian." If anyone took notice of it, they kept it to themselves.

Meanwhile he was the model of military discipline. Just as he could express his passionate and morbid nature in his controlled verses, he could define himself in terms of a rigid military identity. By 1829, at Fortress Monroe, Virginia, he reached the highest rank possible for an enlisted man, Regimental Sergeant Major.

Restless after two years, he had enough of the army. However, he had signed on for five. In an attempt to gain release, Edgar revealed his true identity to his commanding officer. He then learned the cost of breaking his enlistment. The officer knew John Allan and promised to discharge Edgar on one condition: he had to reconcile with his guardian.

The first attempt received a cool response from John Allan, "He had better remain as he is until the termination of his enlistment." Edgar tried a variety of tactics to manipulate Allan—all went unanswered—until he requested help to enter West Point. The request coincided with the death of Fanny Allan after a long illness.

Fanny never stopped loving Edgar. A reverence to her memory softened John Allan. He allowed Edgar to come home, bought him a mourning suit, and agreed to help him enter West Point.

West Point proved more difficult than Edgar expected, as was his reconciliation with John Allan. The entry process required Edgar to give details on his birth and parentage. He lied. He said he was an orphan, whose parents died in the Richmond Theater fire of 1809. He said John Allan adopted him as "son and heir." John Allan wrote a recommendation letter that was coldly impersonal and clearly stated that Edgar was not a relation. In May, Edgar was placed on a waiting list. He went away hopeful that the list might shrink and he would be admitted in September. If not, perhaps the following June.

Orphaned by two mothers, rejected by two fathers, Edgar searched for any familial anchor. He went to live in Baltimore, reading, writing, and vainly looking for work. As the admission procedure dragged on without result, Allan accused Edgar of misleading him. Edgar tried to appease him, but new clashes over money and his writing opened old wounds.

Foolishly, Edgar asked Allan to guarantee a publisher a sum of money against possible losses if they published his second book of poetry. Angry letters passed back and forth, the last from Allan a virtual prohibition against Edgar returning to Richmond.

In December 1829, without the help of Allan, Edgar's seventy-two page *Al Aaraaf, Tamerlane and Minor Poems by Edgar A. Poe* was finally published in Baltimore. The poems continued to exhibit his mastery of form and express "disillusionment with the world and an escape into some more congenial realm of dream or of the imagination." Aside from one glowing review, the reaction was either indifferent or unfavorable.

In the spring of 1830 came word that Edgar had been admitted to West Point. He roomed with three other cadets and was paid an allowance of $16 a month. His time at West Point would follow the same pattern as his previous experience. He excelled at the class work. His contemporaries reported his usual personality quirks. He continued to write, entertaining his mates with biting satirical verses about their superiors and their shared life. He cultivated a reputation for "humbugs" or practical jokes.

Quickly, though, he wearied of West Point life. After the excesses of university, the undemanding life in the regular army, and a year idly waiting, Edgar felt constricted by the scratchy, ill-fitted uniforms, the crowded and uncomfortable conditions, the roll calls, the drills, the incessant study, the rigid discipline, and the oppressive authority. He was also in debt again, John Allan having insufficiently supplemented Edgar's military stipend.

Edgar decided to resign.

Unfortunately, this could not happen without the permission of John Allan who "flatly refused." Allan assumed Edgar had returned to his capricious and wayward life. Allan also wrote Edgar not to trouble him with any further communication.

Edgar was determined. In the absence of permission, he would obtain a discharge by other means. He stopped going to classes and church. He ignored duties and orders. By the end of January 1831, he stood trial for court martial. He did not defend himself. He was dismissed in February and took a steamboat to New York with twenty-four cents in his pocket.

He wrote Allan that he left without even a cloak to protect him from the winter weather. Again, not true. He kept his cadet's overcoat for the rest of his life.

New York was like no city Edgar had ever seen. He grew up a southerner, in a sedate agricultural society. New York was noisy, hard, busy, and bewildering. He secured meager lodgings near

Madison Square. Destitute, he wrote John Allan for help, with no reply. He wrote the Superintendent of West Point, with no reply. He took up a subscription among his fellow cadets at West Point for the publication of a book of poems.

Eager to see Edgar's scandalous satires in print, the cadets paid seventy-five cents each to underwrite the publication. In April 1831, *Poems by Edgar A. Poe* was published in an edition of five hundred copies and dedicated to "The U.S. Corps of Cadets."

The cadets received the poorly produced volume "with a general expression of disgust." Edgar, again, reprinted his earlier poems with a selection of new ones. There were none of the satires that built his reputation at the Point. Edgar had a knack for alienating anyone who could help him.

These new poems, some of his best, reveal an intense preoccupation with death, dying, and the afterlife. Edgar was working out his grief in his writing. It was not uncharacteristic for the times either. High mortality rates made the Victorian age a time of obsession with death. Graveyard poetry was among the most prolific verse forms of the nineteenth century.

Edgar always considered himself a poet first, declaring, "Poetry has been not a purpose, but a passion." He published half of his poems by age twenty-two. It is one part of his lifelong misfortune that the quality of his poetry was never recognized in his lifetime.

After the failure of *Poems,* he didn't publish another volume of poetry for fourteen years.

THE NARRATIVE

OF

ARTHUR GORDON PYM.

OF NANTUCKET.

COMPRISING THE DETAILS OF A MUTINY AND ATROCIOUS BUTCHERY
ON BOARD THE AMERICAN BRIG GRAMPUS, ON HER WAY TO
THE SOUTH SEAS, IN THE MONTH OF JUNE, 1827.

WITH AN ACCOUNT OF THE RECAPTURE OF THE VESSEL BY THE
SURVIVERS; THEIR SHIPWRECK AND SUBSEQUENT HORRIBLE
SUFFERINGS FROM FAMINE; THEIR DELIVERANCE BY
MEANS OF THE BRITISH SCHOONER JANE GUY; THE
BRIEF CRUISE OF THIS LATTER VESSEL IN THE
ANTARCTIC OCEAN; HER CAPTURE, AND THE
MASSACRE OF HER CREW AMONG A
GROUP OF ISLANDS IN THE

EIGHTY-FOURTH PARALLEL OF SOUTHERN LATITUDE;

TOGETHER WITH THE INCREDIBLE ADVENTURES AND
DISCOVERIES

STILL FARTHER SOUTH

TO WHICH THAT DISTRESSING CALAMITY GAVE RISE.

NEW-YORK:

HARPER & BROTHERS, 82 CLIFF-ST.

1838.

Title page from Edgar's only novel

Act Three
1831 - 1838
Storyteller

BURTON'S

GENTLEMAN'S MAGAZINE,

AND

MONTHLY AMERICAN REVIEW.

EDITED BY WILLIAM E. BURTON,

AND

EDGAR A. POE.

By a gentleman, we mean not to draw a line that would be invidious between high and low, rank and subordination, riches and poverty. No. *The distinction is in the mind.* Whoever is open, just and true; whoever is of a humane and affable demeanor; whoever is honourable in himself, and in his judgment of others, and requires no law but his word to make him fulfil an engagement—such a man is *a gentleman*;—and such a man may be found among the tillers of the earth as well as in the drawing rooms of the high-born and the rich.

De Vaas.

VOLUME VI.

FROM JANUARY TO JULY.

PHILADELPHIA:
WILLIAM E. BURTON,
OPPOSITE THE EXCHANGE, DOCK STREET.
1840

"I do believe God gave me a spark of genius, but He quenched it in Misery."

After three months, twenty-two year old Edgar left New York for Baltimore. He moved into a tiny home with his father's widowed sister, Aunt Maria Clemm. Sharing the home was Edgar's seventy-five year old bedridden grandmother, Maria's two children (thirteen year old Henry and nine year old Virginia) and Edgar's older brother, William Henry.

Aunt Maria offered little help other than shelter. His aunt was barely making ends meet, supplementing her odd jobs of sewing and dressmaking, with begging and borrowing. Perpetually out of work, Edgar repeatedly wrote John Allan for help. Not until almost a year later did Allan send a little more than a week's wages, $20.

During this time, the details of Edgar's personal life are poorly documented. He drank, but most recollections of him are of a moderate drinker. Other acquaintances recalled his good looks, athletic build, and gentlemanly manner. All remember his erratic moody nature. In modern terms, he might be described as bipolar, or the more descriptive "manic-depressive."

He had several failed relationships. Not only had his personality problems thwarted these romances, but also his lack of employment and career prospects. Perhaps this is why he formed such a close attachment to his young cousin, Virginia. With dark hair, violet eyes, and—like his mother—a slight, petite figure, Virginia shared all the characteristics of a "Poe woman."

He tutored her in languages and encouraged her interests in

music. It is likely during this time that Edgar started to fall in love with Virginia, despite her young age. Less a romantic love, it was more an expression of his deep longing for family.

Reuniting with his brother was also a cause for good feelings. William Henry joined the Navy (or the merchant marines) in his teens and traveled the world. Aside from sticking with that commitment, he had much in common with his younger brother. Physically, they both resembled their mother. William Henry wrote and published some twenty stories, poems and sketches. Haunted by the death of their mother, his writing was similar to Edgar in melancholy and despair. It is quite possible they collaborated in writing—identical stanzas appearing in each of their respective poems. William Henry also liked to drink, a lot.

The reunion lasted barely six months as Edgar watched his brother drink himself to death. (Some sources cite cholera as his killer, others tuberculosis.) He died August 1, 1831. He was twenty-four years old, the same age as his mother when she died.

Inspired by his brother and urged on by his newest surrogate mother, Maria, Edgar turned to writing fiction. In the spring of 1831, the *Saturday Courier,* a Philadelphia newspaper, sponsored a $100 contest for the best American tale. He did not win, but the judges took notice. In January 1832, the paper printed Edgar's first published tale, "Metzengerstein," a dreamlike horror story of supernatural revenge. Within the year, four of his comic tales were published. By modern standards, Edgar was a poor humorist. Nevertheless, the stories are remarkable for their variety of subject and technique and all have the central underlying theme of surviving death.

In June 1833, the Baltimore *Saturday Visiter* offered two prizes: $50 for best story and $25 for best poem. Edgar submitted a new poem and six tales. His story, "MS. In a Bottle," a sea faring adventure that builds a sustaining dread in the face of imminent catastrophe, won the prize. The judges praised all of his stories, "these tales are eminently distinguished by a wild, vigorous, and poetical imagination, a rich style, a fertile invention, and varied and curious learning."

Edgar felt he should have also won the poetry prize. One of the judges confirmed that they gave the prize to the second best poem because they didn't want to award both to the same person. Edgar resented it even more when he found out that the editor of the paper, John Hewitt, wrote the winning poem under a pseudonym.

One of the judges in the contest was John Pendleton Kennedy, a successful lawyer and author. He became Edgar's first literary patron and a surrogate father. He found Edgar in a state of starvation, bought him clothing, and advised him on the publication of a collection of his recent stories.

On March 27, 1834, his foster father, John Allan, died. If Edgar was still hoping for any inheritance, none was forthcoming. "I am thrown entirely upon my own resources," he told Kennedy, "with no profession, and very few friends." At the time, Edgar was one of the very few authors trying to make a living at writing. American authors were at a disadvantage, because publishers favored authors from England. There were no copyright laws and the English books could be pirated and reprinted at no cost. It is estimated that the total income from all of Edgar's books, over twenty years, was about $300.

Realizing his desperate need, Kennedy recommended Edgar to Thomas W. White, the publisher of *Southern Literary Messenger.* "He is very clever with his pen—classical and scholar-like. He wants experience and direction, but I have no doubt he can be very useful to you."

Better education and the proliferation of printing presses led to an explosion of magazine publishing in America. Thomas White, a Richmond printer, began to publish the *Messenger*, a monthly magazine of sixty-four, double-column, pages in August 1834. The magazine contained essays, sentimental stories, and mediocre poetry. White wrote in the first issue that the journal intended, "to stimulate the pride and genius of the South, and awaken from its long slumber the literary exertion of this portion of the country."

He published Edgar's first story, "Bernice," in March 1835. White criticized the tale of terror as "too horrible." Edgar agreed. He went on to say that the most successful stories contained "ludicrous heightened into the grotesque: the fearful colored into the horrible: the witty exaggerated into the burlesque: the singular wrought out into the strange and mystical." He continued that, "To be appreciated, you must be read."

These are the principles Edgar followed the rest of his career. He had an instinctive understanding of what would attract and hold the attention of the reading public.

As a result of their correspondence, White asked 25 year old Edgar to come to Richmond and join the magazine. It was his first prospect of prolonged paid employment in years. His salary was $60 a month. While White traveled to sell subscriptions, Edgar handled all the operations to publish the magazine, from writing most of the articles, to binding up, and addressing the issues.

It would not take long for a crisis to throw Edgar deep into depression. Maria Clemm wrote that his cousin Neilson Poe was ready to take in and educate her daughter Virginia at his own expense. Edgar panicked at the thought of losing this connection with his surrogate mother and the young girl he planned to marry. Neilson, whom Edgar called his "bitterest enemy," knew of his attachment to Virginia and disapproved of the prospect of their marriage. He begged her to remain loyal.

He wrote a hysterical letter to Maria and Virginia: "I'm blinded with tears while I write this letter, my last, my last, my only hold on life is cruelly torn away. I have no desire to live—and will not. I love—you know I love—Virginia, passionately, devotedly."

As the storm lingered, Edgar turned to the bottle and was fired. White wrote to a friend that Edgar "is unfortunately rather dissipated, and therefore I can place very little reliance upon him." One of the printers working for him recalled, "Mr. Poe was a fine gentleman when he was sober. He was ever kind and courtly, and at such times, everyone liked him. But when he was drinking he was about one of the most disagreeable men I have ever met."

In September, Edgar raced to Baltimore.

White, concerned for his welfare, wrote a frank, almost fatherly letter. He doubted Edgar's promises to reform, warned him about the evils of alcohol, offered to help his reform from the vice in his own household, and agreed to reinstate him if he separated himself from the bottle.

By October, the crisis ended. Edgar had persuaded the

Clemms to reject Neilson's offer and allow him to become responsible for them. It is speculated that he secretly married the thirteen-year-old Virginia. He convinced White to rehire him. Edgar moved his new family to Richmond.

By December, White officially appointed Edgar editor of the *Messenger.* He prospered. He gave up drinking and wrote Kennedy that his health was better than it was in years past. He had also been writing, but mostly as editor and critic. In his fourteen-year magazine writing career, Edgar wrote close to 1,000 essays, reviews, articles, columns, and critical notices.

Since the inclusion of "Bernice," he had contributed other tales and essays. The need to produce a massive amount of copy now intensified his output. He published critical reviews of nineteen books, published old stories, and six new ones, including "The Unparalleled Adventure of One Hans Pfaall." Not one of Edgar's best stories, the character, Hans Pfaall, constructs a helium-based balloon contraption that he flies to the moon. It is the first instance of Edgar using the device of an imaginary voyage as a way to explore human psychology.

Thirty years before the writings of Jules Verne, the story is among the earliest examples of the genre of science fiction. Influenced by several Poe stories, Verne retold the Hans Pfaall as *From Earth to the Moon* and "The Balloon Hoax" as *Around the World in Eighty Days.* He also wrote a sequel to *The Narrative of Arthur Gordon Pym,* entitled *The Sphinx of Ice,* continuing the story where Edgar left off.

His reviews provoked the most attention. The reputations of some of the most fashionable writers did not emerge unscathed from Edgar's fine critical mind and sharp wit. He was irritable and even savage in his critiques. In one review from 1836 he wrote, "This book is a public imposition. It should have been printed among the quack advertisements in a spare corner of the newspaper." He wanted to impose his modern sensibilities on the stale literature of the times. He also disliked bias for northern writers that dominated the press.

He desired a reputation. He wanted fame. He needed to make an impression. He set the national standard for book reviewing. He held high standards and refused to abide second-rate books. He would end up paying a heavy price for his candor. He made enemies of many authors, other critics, and the publishers that profited from both.

Edgar's meager salary allowed him to provide the Clemms with minimal comforts. They provided the family stability that enabled him to write. On May 16, 1836, after living together in Richmond for seven months, the twenty-seven year old Edgar officially married his fourteen-year-old cousin. A witness swore the petite bride was twenty-one and the minister made no objection.

Wedded bliss was fleeting and by the end of the year, Edgar sabotaged himself again. The strains of the magazine weighed on him. Ignoring White's warnings, he rejoined the bottle. The drinking wasn't constant, but he went on binges. It made him incapable of doing his work and brought out the negative side of his personality. In December 1836, White dismissed him.

Three weeks later, White wrote to a friend that the *Messenger* "shall outlive all the injury it has sustained from Mr. Poe's management." White was jealous of Edgar and felt the magazine was no longer his own. To allay his own ego, he lied. The magazine sustained no injury at all. Under Edgar's supervision, the magazine attracted more notice and more praise than at any time in its history. The circulation had risen from 700 to 3,500 subscribers. In addition, it had published some of the finest American stories ever written. Edgar was a brilliant editor and, perhaps, the greatest prose writer in the country at the time.

Following his pattern of moving to a new city after a disastrous experience, Edgar began again in New York. He was just in time for the "Panic of 1837," one of the worst depressions in American history. He found it impossible to find work. He only sold two stories in this period. The literary establishment closed their doors to the man who challenged them. The family survived; often forced to live on bread and molasses for weeks.

At the beginning of 1838, they tried their luck in Philadelphia. His choice may have been no coincidence; Philadelphia was the publishing center of America. His early employment is not known other than he picked up odd jobs as a journalistic hack, writing filler and criticisms to order. He wrote to a friend for any job rather than, "the miserable life of literary drudgery to which I now, with breaking heart, submit, and for which neither my temper nor my abilities have fitted me."

That summer Harper and Brothers published his first, and only, novel, *The Narrative of Arthur Gordon Pym.* Years later, he would call it "a very silly book." While not his best work, he was his harshest critic. The book received good, but mixed reviews and was not a financial success.

He made money in any way possible. Thomas Wyatt wished to

release an abridged version of his book, *Manual of Conchology.* His publisher disagreed. So, he hired Edgar to condense the book, supply his name, as author, and write a new Preface and Introduction. For *The Conchologist's First Book,* Wyatt paid Edgar $50.

It was the only book under his name to go into a second printing in his lifetime.

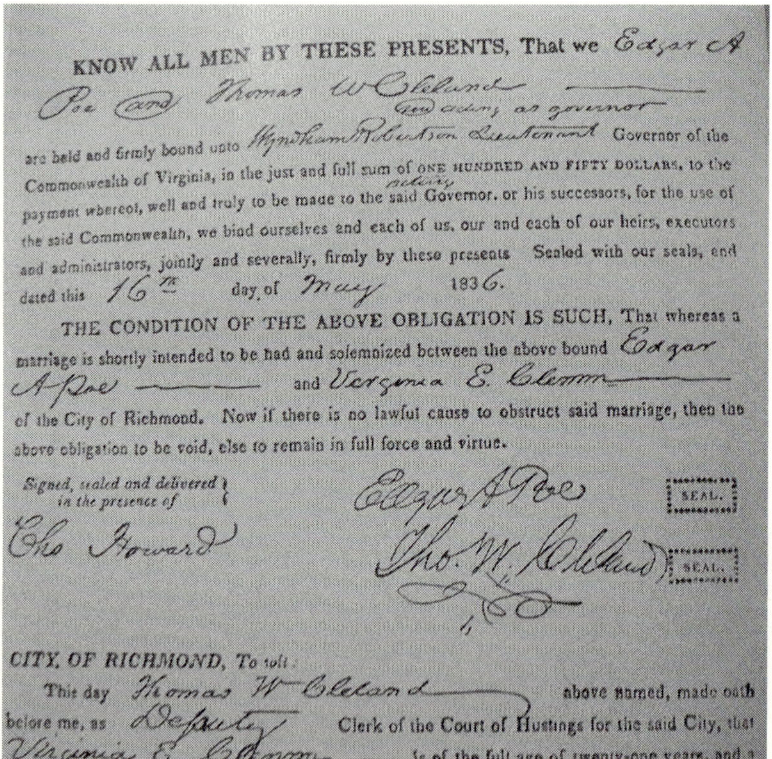
KNOW ALL MEN BY THESE PRESENTS, That we Edgar A Poe and Thomas W Cleland — acting as governor are held and firmly bound unto Wyndham Robertson Lieutenant Governor of the Commonwealth of Virginia, in the just and full sum of ONE HUNDRED AND FIFTY DOLLARS, to the payment whereof, well and truly to be made to the said acting Governor, or his successors, for the use of the said Commonwealth, we bind ourselves and each of us, our and each of our heirs, executors and administrators, jointly and severally, firmly by these presents. Sealed with our seals, and dated this 16th day of May 1836.

THE CONDITION OF THE ABOVE OBLIGATION IS SUCH, That whereas a marriage is shortly intended to be had and solemnized between the above bound Edgar A Poe — and Virginia E. Clemm — of the City of Richmond. Now if there is no lawful cause to obstruct said marriage, then the above obligation to be void, else to remain in full force and virtue.

Signed, sealed and delivered in the presence of
Chs Howard

Edgar A Poe [SEAL.]
Tho. W. Cleland [SEAL.]

CITY, OF RICHMOND, To wit:

This day Thomas W Cleland above named, made oath before me, as Deputy Clerk of the Court of Hustings for the said City, that Virginia E Clemm — is of the full age of twenty-one years, and a resident of the said City. Given under my hand, this 16 day of May 1836

Chs Howard

Edgar and Virginia's marriage certificate

Act Four
1839 - 1844
American Genius

THE

CONCHOLOGIST'S FIRST BOOK:

OR,

A SYSTEM

OF

TESTACEOUS MALACOLOGY,

Arranged expressly for the use of Schools,

IN WHICH

THE ANIMALS, ACCORDING TO CUVIER, ARE GIVEN WITH THE SHELLS,

A GREAT NUMBER OF NEW SPECIES ADDED,

AND THE WHOLE BROUGHT UP, AS ACCURATELY AS POSSIBLE, TO THE PRESENT CONDITION OF THE SCIENCE.

BY EDGAR A. POE.

WITH ILLUSTRATIONS OF TWO HUNDRED AND FIFTEEN SHELLS, PRESENTING A CORRECT TYPE OF EACH GENUS.

PHILADELPHIA:

PUBLISHED FOR THE AUTHOR, BY

HASWELL, BARRINGTON, AND HASWELL,

AND FOR SALE BY THE PRINCIPAL BOOKSELLERS IN THE UNITED STATES.

1839.

"I could not love except where Death
was mingling his with Beauty's breath."

In the two and a half years since his dismissal from the *Messenger,* Edgar earned only $193 including the recent $50 (the equivalent of a month's wages) from the conchology book. In May 1839, Edgar finally found an opportunity for a steady income. He approached William Burton for an assistant editor's position on the staff of *Burton's Gentlemen's Magazine.*

William Burton was a high living comic actor and entrepreneur from England. His magazine published the standard mix of light, entertaining articles: poems, fiction, and essays. Burton needed help because his acting tours took him away from Philadelphia. Although not an ideal match, Edgar accepted the meager $10 a week he was offered to survive. It was a match doomed from the start.

Edgar's duties included proofreading, compiling short fillers, preparing manuscripts for the press, and supervising the printing. Burton treated Edgar as no more than a servant. He fought against Edgar's caustic book reviews, which led to a major argument before the end of the first month.

Edgar's position gave him a new outlet for his stories; which he was paid an extra $3 a page. His work was seen as modern, ahead of its time, and unique. An article in the *St. Louis Bulletin* remarked, "There are few writers in the country—take Neal, Irving, and Willis away and we would say *none*—who can compete successfully in many respects, with Poe."

Edgar deserved the praise. *Burton's* published some of his best work, among them "The Fall of the House of Usher" and "William Wilson."

"The Fall of the House of Usher" has become an enduring classic of horror. It encapsulates all of Edgar's characteristic preoccupations: a gloomy landscape, a crumbling mansion, a sorrowful somber atmosphere, a terrified narrator, a debilitated man, a tubercular woman, arcane books, premature burial, oppressive secrets, turbulent weather, the supernatural, a return from the grave, and a fated doom.

"William Wilson" is a classic psychological thriller based on an idea by Washington Irving. A story of supernatural duality, William Wilson is tormented by a mysterious masked figure who turns out to be the physical twin of himself, including sharing the same name.

In 1839, the growing notoriety of these stories enabled him to publish a collection of twenty-five stories, a two-volume edition titled, *Tales of the Grotesque and Arabesque.* The "grotesque" tales were comedic or satire; the "arabesque" were serious, imaginative, and poetic.

There were some mixed reviews, but most were positive. *Alexander's Weekly Messenger* called the tales a "playful effusion of remarkable and powerful intellect." Other papers praised his writing as "unusually excellent"; "some of the most popular tales of American origin"; and "one of the most extraordinary narratives ever penned." For some it established Edgar on the national literary scene: "To say we have *read* this production attentively is not enough. We have *studied* it . . . He has placed himself in the foremost rank of American writers."

The state of publishing was such that Edgar was not paid royalties. He retained the copyright and received twenty-five free copies to distribute. The company printed 750 copies and for taking the risk, kept all profits. Despite the positive reviews, the public didn't rush to buy. It took three years to sell out.

In May 1840, Burton put the magazine up for sale. Figuring he would need a job soon, Edgar began planning a magazine of his own. Burton fired him. This ignited Edgar's usual bitter war of words, both real and unfounded, between the two men. Edgar and Burton split after one year of association. As would happen in only the lowest points of his life, he returned to binge drinking.

In October 1840, Burton sold his magazine to George Graham, publisher of *The Casket,* for $3,500.

Edgar was sick for a month starting in December and lasting into January. His magazine dreams were delayed temporarily. The delays increased and became permanent. He tried twice more, in 1843 and 1845, to start magazines, but the dream of owning his own periodical was never truly realized.

In February 1841, Graham hired Edgar as editor at a salary of $800 a year. He was now being paid $300 more a year than with *Burton's* and had an assistant editor to handle the routine drudgery of the business.

Graham was a shrewd businessman and a hard worker. He was gracious, friendly, and liberal with what he paid his authors—less so with his editors. He combined the two magazines into *Graham's Lady's and Gentlemen's Magazine,* with combined subscribers of 5,000.

The magazine was high quality, with expensive engravings, and fiction by well-known authors. The magazine also ran essays on art, nature, and current interests. It was not controversial and had a strong moral tone. *Graham's* even tried to draw a female market with articles on "domestic" matters. It fit Edgar poorly, but he tried to stick with it—for a while.

At home, Edgar was the picture of domestic tranquility. He was debt free for the first and only time in his life. Lower middle-class, he entertained visitors in his cramped, but well-appointed home. He showed off the new harp and piano that he bought for Virginia. They would play games. Once while playing "leap frog" in the garden, he split his pants much to his embarrassment and Virginia's laughter. He described her as happy and full of life. After his workday ended, he would sit at home writing.

At work, Edgar was productive. He continued his crusades through the literary landscape, taking no prisoners. In these years, he matured as a critic, defining the role as the mediator between a work of genius and an uneducated public. He further refined his literary theories, especially on the structure and purpose of the short story.

His most successful magazine articles were a series on cryptography, in which he explained the construction of secret codes, created word puzzles, and solved puzzles sent in by readers. This boosted circulation and Edgar acquired fame as an analytical and mathematical genius. Also popular was his articles on "autography," what we think of now as graphology. He would develop a character reading from a signature sent in by a reader.

These puzzling deductions lead directly to Edgar writing some his most important works. In *Graham's,* he published three "tales of ratiocination," or logical reasoning, with a central "detective" hero. (The word "detective" did not exist in the English language until 1843, two years after Edgar's stories.) "The Murders in the Rue Morgue" and "The Purloined Letter," were set in Paris and featured C. Auguste Dupin. The third story, "The Gold-Bug," was set on Sullivan Island in North Carolina and featured William Legrand.

These weren't just any detective stories, these are widely recognized as the first detective stories. While Edgar is acknowledged as a genius who changed literature in far reaching ways, what is lost is that, particularly in his magazine writing, he had strong commercial senses. He saw the popularity of crime writing in the newspapers and "penny dreadfuls" then applied his brilliance to it. Although, in his time, he downplayed the stories' popularity saying they were just novelties.

"The Rue Morgue" created the classic formula of detective fiction. Detectives Sherlock Holmes and Hercule Poirot (two of many examples) are direct descendants of Dupin. Edgar's story includes a Watson-like narrator, a locked room mystery, an eccentric, but brilliant detective, bumbling police, scientific analysis of evidence, systematic interrogation of suspects, and the gathering of the suspects to deliver the final speech naming the culprit.

In April 1841, the month he published "The Rue Morgue," Edgar met Rufus Griswold, a powerful literary journalist who later became a dangerous enemy. Griswold combined endless energy with a considerable lack of talent. A career opportunist, he amassed his literary power by compiling a series of popular anthologies of poetry and stories.

In many ways, his personality mirrored Edgar's. He was caustic, hypersensitive, erratic, dour, and savagely vindictive. They suppressed their mutual dislike and presented a façade of friendship to each other. Edgar wanted to be included in Griswold's anthologies. Griswold wanted Edgar's critical praise. Early in their relationship, Edgar wrote that Griswold was "a gentleman of fine taste and sound judgment." Later, he would write that his talents were "of a mediocre character," and "he will be quoted as the unfaithful servant who abused his trust." The latter became an eerily precise prediction.

Meanwhile, *Graham's* prospered. Under Edgar's editorial hand, the circulation increased from 5,000 to 40,000 issues. His contributions to the magazine increased his reputation as a fearless critic and master of gothic horror. Pleased with the image, he compared himself several times to a magician; as if the wave of hand would create a successful magazine.

Still, he was dissatisfied personally and struggling financially. He discovered his popularity did not translate to literary power, when he tried and failed to get an updated collection of his stories published. He felt the magazine was too bland. He complained, given the sevenfold increase in readership, that he had not received a raise. Graham also paid him less for his freelance work than other authors received for theirs. Edgar, as usual, disliked Graham's editorial interference. Edgar said that he had been "forced to model my thoughts at the will of men whose imbecility was evident to all but themselves."

Then, on the evening of January 20, 1842, Virginia Poe was singing at the piano when she began coughing up blood. A burst blood vessel. Tuberculosis. The "white plague," as it was sometimes called, tallied up to one quarter of all deaths in the nineteenth century. For two weeks, Virginia was dangerously ill, and Edgar thought she might die. This began a cycle of recovery and relapse that tortured Edgar for five years. He had disabling bouts of ill health himself, coupled with fitful bouts of boozing as well.

In April 1842, Edgar resigned from the magazine. In light of Virginia's illness and the debt they incurred, it couldn't have happened at a worst time. However, all the usual resentments boiled over. After he returned from one of his "absences," he found another man sitting in his editor's chair. Within months, Rufus Griswold would take his place at a higher salary.

Edgar agonized. He borrowed money when he could. He tried to get several government jobs, but always frustrated his own efforts or any efforts on his behalf.

Throughout the first half of the 1840s, he continued to publish some of his finest writing: "The Masque of Red Death," "The Pit and the Pendulum," "The Black Cat," and "The Tell-Tale Heart."

In the autumn of 1843, Edgar told a fellow writer in Philadelphia that "his wife and Mrs. Clemm were starving." In search of income, on November 21, he began a career as a lecturer with a talk entitled "Poetry in America." The hall in which he spoke was packed, hundreds of people were unable to gain admission. He repeated the lecture in Wilmington, Baltimore, and New York.

As a lecturer, Edgar had presence. From the newspaper accounts, he was an accomplished orator and master rhetorician. They praised his eloquent delivery and wonderful reading voice. While he had a reputation as a severe critic, the papers commented on his ability to strike a balance between his severity and impartiality in his speeches.

For two hours, Edgar delivered his opinions on American literary politics, the poetry it produced, and the function of criticism. His main target was Rufus Griswold. He said that Griswold's anthology, *Poets and Poetry of America,* was the "best" of the current compilations, but then made a personal attack on the man. He revealed to his audiences that Griswold was a tasteless New Englander, unashamed puffer, and follower of the herd. He chose much of the poetry because of friendship, not quality.

Wounded, Griswold eventually took revenge after Edgar's death, and engaged in "the most lethal character assassination in the history of American literature."

By April 1844, Edgar uprooted his family and moved to New York. The fact that his previous experiences there had been almost completely unhappy did not deter him. Under all of Edgar's turmoil, there was an unextinguished flame of hope.

Act Five
1844 - 1848
Dark Days

SUN OFFICE
April 13, 10 o'clock A. M.

ASTOUNDING NEWS!

BY EXPRESS VIA NORFOLK!

THE

ATLANTIC CROSSED

IN

THREE DAYS!

SIGNAL TRIUMPH

OF

MR. MONCK MASON'S

FLYING

MACHINE!!!

Arrival at Sullivan's Island, near Charleston, S. C., of Mr. Mason, Mr. Robert Holland, Mr Henson, Mr. Harrison Ainsworth, and four others, in the

STEERING BALLOON

"VICTORIA,"

AFTER A PASSAGE OF

SEVENTY-FIVE HOURS

FROM LAND TO LAND.

FULL PARTICULARS

OF THE

VOYAGE!!!

The great problem is at length solved. The air, as well as the earth and the ocean, has been

"I became insane with long intervals of horrible sanity"

Needing income, Edgar controlled his drinking and churned out hackwork for a variety of newspapers. He became the New York correspondent for a small Pennsylvania newspaper called the *Columbia Spy.* He dashed off small articles for the Philadelphia *Public Ledger,* the *Columbian Magazine,* the *Democratic Review,* and others.

Through the years, Edgar carried out several "humbugs" or practical jokes. Many of his hoaxes were so realistic, that they were later quoted in textbooks and encyclopedias. A week after his arrival in New York, he sold to the New York *Sun* a hoax trumpeting the crossing of the Atlantic Ocean in three days by balloon. "The Balloon-Hoax" was a realistic improvement over his earlier story of a balloon trip to the moon.

On April 13, the newspaper carried the headline: ASTOUNDING INTELLIGENCE BY PRIVATE EXPRESS FROM CHARLESTON VIA NORFOLK! THE ATLANTIC OCEAN CROSSED IN THREE DAYS! ARRIVAL AT SULLIVAN'S ISLAND OF A STEERING BALLOON INVENTED BY MR. MONCK MASON!!

As Edgar described it, the story caused a sensation: "On the morning of its announcement, the whole square surrounding the *Sun* building was literally besieged, blocked up—ingress and egress being alike impossible, for a period soon after sunrise until about two o'clock P.M. . . .I never witnessed more intense excitement to get possession of a newspaper. As soon as the first few copies made their way into the streets, they were bought up, at almost any price, from the news-boys, who made a profitable speculation." Edgar received his usual meager fee for the story, but did not share in the profits of this short-lived success.

Nearly a decade previous, the *Sun*, needing a boost in circulation, perpetrated "The Moon Hoax." In 1835, the paper printed a series of stories about an astronomer who spotted life on the moon with his telescope. The *Sun* became the most read newspaper in the country and the story was reprinted around the world. The competing newspapers in town, recognizing Edgar's balloon story as a similar hoax, exposed it to the public. Within a couple of days, the *Sun* printed a retraction. Edgar's reputation took another hit.

The sum total of all of his work was still barely enough for his small family to live on. The only steady outlet for articles was the New York *Evening Mirror.* By October 1844, *Mirror* editor Nathaniel P. Willis offered Edgar a position at the paper for $750 a year as assistant editor and "mechanical paragraphist." Edgar badly needed the money. He liked Willis enough, so he accepted. Willis later wrote, "It was his business to sit at a desk, in a corner of the editorial room, ready to be called upon for any of the miscellaneous work at the moment—announcing news, condensing statements, answering correspondents, noticing amusements—everything but the writing of the 'leader,' or constructing any article upon which his peculiar idiosyncrasy of mind could be impressed."

It was a huge step down for the former editor of several major magazines. After Edgar's death, Willis recollected him fondly and defended him against Rufus Griswold's slanders, "We had seen but one presentment of the man,—a quiet, patient, industrious, and most gentlemanly person, commanding the utmost respect and good feeling by his unvarying deportment and ability." He also reflected on "the presence and magnetism of a man of genius" and Edgar's "mysterious electricity of mind." Willis added though, "he was a man who never smiled."

Early in 1845, Edgar did have something to smile about. He was thrilled by his newest poem, so much so that when he met fellow author William Ross Wallace on the street, he could not contain his enthusiasm.

"Wallace," said Edgar, "I have just written the greatest poem that ever was written."

"Have you?" said Wallace. "That is a fine achievement."

"Would you like to hear it?" said Edgar.

"Most certainly," said Wallace.

Edgar then read the soon to be famous verses. When he finished it, he turned to Wallace for his approval.

"Poe—they are fine; uncommonly fine." Wallace said.

"Fine?" Edgar sputtered. "Is that all you can say for this poem? I tell you it's the greatest poem that was ever written."

Many would hail "The Raven" as just that—the greatest. Published first in the *American Review* and reprinted in a few more newspapers, "The Raven" became a sensation. Soon everyone was saying "Nevermore." It became a catchword much like "Dy-no-mite!" in the 1970s or "Whaaaaat's uuuuuuup" in the 1990s. Actors incorporated the word into their dialogue to automatic laughter and applause. The poem's rhythm made it an ideal choice for school texts on elocution and public speaking. Its popularity made it ripe for dozens of parodies. Suddenly, Edgar was the most famous poet in America.

The poem was influenced by two works that Edgar critically reviewed, the structure and internal rhymes from Elizabeth Barrett's poem, "Lady Geraldine's Courtship," and the central image of the ominous raven from Charles Dickens' *Barnaby Ridge.* The poem tells the dramatic story of a man mourning the death of a woman he loved, and is visited by a bird of ill omen; whose presence increases his loneliness and depression. Edgar explained the action more simply in "The Philosophy of Composition": "A raven having learned by rote the single word 'Nevermore,' and having escaped from the custody of its owner, is driven at midnight, through the violence of a storm, to seek admission at a window from which a light still gleams—the chamber window of a student, occupied half in pouring over a volume, half in dreaming of a beloved mistress deceased." Specifically he described the black bird as an evocation of "Mournful and Never-ending Remembrance."

The poem can also be seen as a commentary on Edgar's life at the time, the looming loss of his beloved Virginia. As the narrator of the poem has lost his beloved Lenore, but tortures himself that she may somehow be reclaimed.

At worst, the poem is derided as being empty, all style and no substance. He particularly used the mournful long "o" sound throughout. Nevermore was actually an evolution of Edgar's. He wrote "Lenore" in 1831; he used "no more" in "Silence" (1840);

"evermore" in "The Conqueror Worm" (1843); and finally "nevermore" in "The Raven."

At best, The *New York Express* wrote it surpassed "anything that has been done even by the best poets of the age." The *Richmond Examiner* proclaimed it to have "taken rank over the whole world of literature." The *New World* simply said it was "wild and shivery."

One contemporary wrote of Edgar, "Everyone wants to know him," then added, "but only a very few people seem to get well acquainted with him." With his new found notoriety, he revitalized his speaking career, returning to his "American Poets and Poetry" speech. He cut out his attack on Griswold, but added in an attack on the poet Longfellow, who he accused of plagiarism. The one sided battle (Longfellow had little to say publicly or privately on the matter) was one of the most famous literary feuds in American literary history. Eventually, the conflict became one of the main drivers of the vilification of Edgar in literary circles and the press.

Meanwhile, he enjoyed his celebrity. He could always be prevailed on to recite the poem in his own particular and mournful manner. He "would turn down the lamps till the room was almost dark, then standing in the center of the apartment he would recite those wonderful lines in the most melodious of voices . . . So marvelous was his power as a reader that the auditors would be afraid to draw a breath lest the enchanted spell be broken."

He rejoined the elite literary society. He spent much of his time with the "Blue Stocking Society," a group of female poets. Elizabeth Smith said that Edgar "did not affect the society of men, rather that of highly intellectual women . . . Men were intolerant of all this, but women fell under his fascination and listened in silence." They recognized his need for female attention. In these passionate, but platonic, relationships the women wanted to protect Edgar from himself, nourish his genius, and inspire his art. In other words, mother him.

In turn, Edgar was truly interested in them, some romantically, some for their writings. He saw himself as a mentor and promoter of their talents. He was a patron of female writers in an age when most men were just patronizing.

In the glow of success, Edgar left his position at the *Evening Mirror* and joined the rival *Broadway Journal.* There he republished his earlier stories and poems. He continued his rapier sharp attacks on just about anyone who dared to write. He also became an equally cutting theatrical critic. One theater manager withdrew Edgar's name from the list of complimentary tickets saved for critics after a particularly vicious review of his company's play.

Overworked and underpaid, living on the edge of poverty, Virginia's slow steady decline toward death, and the chaos of his celebrity overwhelmed Edgar and broke his temporary sobriety. The drinking led to embarrassing public outbursts, missed speaking engagements, and disastrous performances.

At the magazine, he repeated the same pattern, which destroyed his previous positions. His partner, Charles Briggs was at first enthusiastic about Edgar, but as the drinking impinged on business, he tried to force Edgar out. By August, Briggs was out maneuvered and was himself forced to leave.

By October 1845, the publisher, John Bisco, sold the

magazine to Edgar for $50. He was the sole proprietor and owner for two months. The death of the *Broadway Journal* was one of the saddest events in Edgar's life.

Edgar had no business sense; as his fame increased, his income declined. He received twenty-three free copies for *Tales* in 1840. The contest-winning story, "The Gold-Bug," sold over 300,000 copies for which he was paid only the original $100 prize money. He received only $9 for the endlessly reprinted "Raven." He never found another steady job after 1845. Without a regular place to publish, he wrote and earned less. His total income would be $288 in 1847, $166 in 1848, and $275 in 1849. ($600 was the bare minimum he needed to survive.)

On January 3, 1846, Edgar published his final farewell: "Unexpected engagements demanding my whole attention, and the objects being fulfilled, so far as regards myself personally, for which the *Broadway Journal* was established, I now, as its Editor, bid farewell—as cordially to foes as to friends."

During the last years of his life, as his physical and mental health began to break down, he was burdened by a series of personal disasters. Sensing the weakness, and the lessened ability to retaliate, the numerous enemies he made through the years publicized his drunkenness and branded his behavior as insane.

As early as April 1846, the St. Louis *Reveille* wrote: "A rumor is in circulation in New York, to the effect that Mr. Edgar A. Poe, the poet and author, has been deranged, and his friends are about to place him under the charge of Dr. Brigham, of the Insane Retreat at Utica." Even the Blue Stocking poets abandoned him after he was the center of a jealous feud between members, Fanny

Osgood and Elizabeth Ellet.

From May to October, Edgar wrote a series of controversial essays on "The Literati of New York City" for *Godey's Lady's Book.* These were gossipy personal descriptions and Edgar's frank opinions of the literary merits of many of the authors that turned their backs on him. It caused a sensation and all the issues sold out. His attacks inevitably provoked retaliation. It all played out publicly in the press with Edgar's reputation getting the worst of it.

One such feud, with Thomas Dunn English, led to a protracted libel suit, in which Edgar prevailed. English accused Edgar of forgery and obtaining money under false pretenses. Edgar sued. He was awarded $225 for damages.

This whole time Edgar was often ill, dreadfully poor, and deeply depressed. As the cold weather arrived, Virginia's health deteriorated rapidly. On December 30, 1846, some well-intentioned friends placed an announcement in the New York *Morning Express* that was eerily reminiscent of his mother's final notice thirty-five years earlier.

"ILLNESS OF EDGAR A. POE.—We regret to learn that this gentlemen and his wife arc both dangerously ill with the consumption, and that the hand of misfortune lies heavily upon their temporal affairs. We are sorry to mention the fact that they are so far reduced as to be barely able to obtain the necessaries of life. That is, indeed, a hard lot, and we do hope that the friends and admirers of Mr. Poe will come promptly to his assistance in his bitterest hour of need."

Death by tuberculosis is a terrible one. As the bacteria

attacked Virginia's tissues, puss filled tubercles formed and caused lesions in her lungs. The disease slowly progressed from lesions to necrosis; from necrosis to erosion; and then bleeding into the lungs. She began to drown in her own blood. Fits of coughing ensued. They became so violent that portions of the lungs were actually coughed out, a slow death by degrees. Each day she was able to draw less and less breath.

On January 29, 1847, Virginia died. Unable to provide proper food, housing, and warmth, Edgar felt humiliated. Undoubtedly hastening the death of his beloved wife, he was tormented with guilt. At twenty-four years old, she died at the same age, and from the same disease, as his mother.

Virginia's death sent Edgar adrift.

In the months following, Edgar's health worsened and he teetered on the edge of madness. He cared little if he lived or died. He lived in a state of inebriation. He only survived due to the ministrations of two women: his Aunt Maria Clemm and Loui Shew, a family friend and nurse.

Most of 1847 was lost. He wrote little, but the experience of Virginia's death produced some haunting new poems like "Ulalume" and "Annabel Lee" and the descent into madness, which was "The Bells." Although as brilliant as these poems appear today, they were rejected repeatedly before he was able to sell them.

As the final days of 1847 approached, Edgar resolved to rebuild his life. Using his imagination as defense against a pitiless world, he finished a speculative philosophical book, *Eureka: A Prose Poem.* He attempted to explain his beliefs on the nature of

God, the nature of the universe, and man's relationship to them. He came to regard it as the culmination of his life's work. The publisher paid $14 for the rights. It sold poorly.

At the same time, he was more desperate for love than ever before. For a time in 1847, he pursued his nurse, Loui Shew. Rebuffed, he returned to Fanny Osgood, who would die of consumption in 1850. During most of 1848, he unsuccessfully pursued four women, more or less at the same time. Often writing each the exact same letters and poems, only changing the dedications.

On November 4, he went to Providence to visit one of the women and await her decision on whether to marry him. Poe's emotional state cracked from the weight of his desperate attempts. The next day, he bought two ounces of laudanum and took a train to Boston, where in a hotel room he ingested half of the drug in a suicide attempt. When he went to mail his farewell letter, a friend noticed his debilitated state and aided him.

Devastated by his failed romances, Edgar began 1849 in practically the same desperate shape he had begun the previous year.

Act Six
1849
Never-ending Remembrance

Daguerreotype of Edgar taken shortly before his death 1849
(Library of Congress)

"I stand amid the roar
Of a surf-tormented shore,
And I hold within my hand
Grains of golden sand-
How few! yet how they creep
Through my fingers to the deep,
While I weep- while I weep!"

Edgar was restless the last year of his life. While courting, lecturing, visiting, and drinking, he moved between New York, Lowell, Philadelphia, Richmond, Norfolk, and Baltimore. His heath and moods fluctuated wildly.

On June 29, 1849, Edgar boarded a steamboat that would take him to Philadelphia and then on to Richmond for a series of lectures. His Aunt Maria saw him off and later recounted his farewell, "God Bless you, my own darling mother. Do not fear for Eddy! See how good I will be while I am away from you, and will come back to love and comfort you." They would be the last words he would speak to her. She would not see him again.

Arriving in Philadelphia, he began drinking and lost the trunk that contained his speeches. A couple of days later, he turned up at the art studio of a friend, John Sartain. He said Edgar looked "pale and haggard, with a wild and frightened expression in his eyes." He also believed Edgar was delusional and suicidal.

When he wrote to his Aunt later, Edgar said he had been ill, perhaps with cholera. He described spasms, violent retching, and weakness. There is some evidence that he may have been suffering from delirium tremens after alcohol poisoning, which also brought on hallucinations and paranoia.

On July 10, he recovered sufficiently enough to find his lost trunk at the train station and borrowed money from Sartain to finish his trip.

In Richmond, Edgar reunited with his sister, Rosalie. It moved him into a better mood. He controlled his failings and toured the area giving lectures. The papers rewarded him with glowing reviews. The *Daily Republican* called the lecture, "one of the richest intellectual we have ever had the good fortune to hear." The *Examiner* wrote that Edgar was "a man of very decided genius."

By September, he successfully courted, and ultimately planned to marry, Elmira Royster, his childhood sweetheart. Deep inside he never stopped loving her, and she felt the same as he did. She hesitated accepting his marriage proposal until he took the temperance pledge, and signed a formal declaration to reform. Her family was less than accepting; her family, particularly her three brothers, deplored the idea of her relationship with such a disreputable man. At least one biographer believes this was the cause of Edgar's demise.

On September 27, Edgar left Richmond by boat for Baltimore. Elmira felt unease at the farewell. He was feverish and his face was ashy. He was entering his final nightmare, sick.

He planned to take a train to Philadelphia for a job editing a book of poetry. It was expected to take couple of days. He would be paid $100. From there he would go to New York to finish some business and to fetch his aunt for his upcoming wedding.

Neilson Poe, living in Baltimore, told Maria that no one knew what happened to Edgar between his arrival on September 28 and his discovery on October 3. The stories of the events of that week slowly appear in the decades following Edgar's dead. The sources are varied, the motives suspicious, and the stories acquire additional details in the retelling.

On the eve of the Congressional elections, was he shanghaied, drugged, and forced to vote repeatedly like so many others? Did he suffer a medical condition? Was it one too many of his binges? On the other hand, two of Edgar's friends, Elizabeth Oakes Smith and Susan Talley hinted it was something else entirely. . .

It is believed Edgar made the Philadelphia train and arrived there in the midafternoon. While he is there something happens that sends his world spiraling. Perhaps, Elmira's brothers caught up with him and tried to intimidate him to stay away from Elmira.

Sometime in the ensuing hours, Edgar would show up at the engraving business of John Sartain. Edgar's arrival would be eerily reminiscent of his visit in the summer, except instead of being suicidal, he was in fear for his life. He urgently asked for a place to hide. He told Sartain that some threatening men were following him. Sartain asked why anyone would want to kill him.

Edgar replied, "It was for revenge."

"Revenge for what?"

"Well, a woman trouble," Edgar mumbled.

He only stayed with Sartain for a night or two. In that time, Edgar asked Sartain to cut off his mustache to change his appearance. He may have furthered the ruse by exchanging his fine and identifiable clothes for some shabby ill-fitting replacements.

He then made his way to his friend George Lippard. He recalled that Edgar was in a severe state of despondency, "poorly clad and with but one shoe on his feet. . ." Edgar needed a loan to get back to Richmond.

Lippard doesn't explain why Edgar needed to get back to Richmond instead of continuing his trip. Perhaps he wanted to get back to the safety of Elmira. Lippard had to borrow the money himself to help Edgar.

Edgar returned to Baltimore on the first leg back to Richmond on or about October 1. He made it no further.

Did the brothers catch up with him? Did they induce him to drink? Did they beat him? At least one theory places the major cause of his death on a head injury. On arrival at the hospital, Edgar's clothing was no longer just shabby, but ripped and soiled.

On October 3, Edgar's friend Joseph Snodgrass received an urgent note from a young printer:

"There is a gentleman, rather worse for wear, at Ryan's Fourth ward polls, who goes under the cognomen of Edgar A. Poe, and who appears in great distress, & he says he is acquainted with you, and I assure, he is in need of immediate assistance."

Snodgrass raced to Gunner's Hall, the location of the Fourth Ward polls, and took Edgar to the hospital at Washington College.

Snodgrass saw that Edgar was dressed in clothing which were clearly not his own. He also noted that Edgar's "face was haggard, not to say bloated, and unwashed, his hair unkempt, and his whole physique repulsive."

Edgar remained at the hospital for three days.

At first, he was confused and incoherent, hot to the touch one moment, cold in another. By noon the next day, he suffered from violent tremors, perhaps another bout of withdrawal. He raved in madness. This went on for twenty hours.

After that period, he recovered some, but was still befuddled.

Suddenly, his violent delirium returned. He struggled with the nurses. He talked to phantasms on the walls. He repeatedly called out the name "Reynolds."

At three A. M. Sunday morning, October 7, Edgar weakened. He rested for a short time. As dawn broke, he briefly woke and, with his last breath, he feebly rasped, "God help my poor soul!"

Edgar A. Poe was dead.

His attending physician, Dr. John Moran, listed the cause of death as "congestion of the brain."

The truth of his death has been speculated on for many years: "brain fever," brain tumor, alcohol poisoning, pneumonia, epilepsy, diabetes, rabies, encephalitis from exposure, are all possible answers. There was no autopsy, so the actual physical cause will remain as mysterious as the circumstances surrounding it.

A family friend paid for "a lead-lined oak casket with an inscribed brass plate at the foot." Neilson Poe paid for the hearse and the carriage that followed it. Only a handful of mourners attended his hastily arranged afternoon burial on October 8, 1849 in the Presbyterian Cemetery. It was a raw and cloudy day.

Two days after his death, Rufus Griswold anonymously published a bitter obituary:

"Edgar Allan Poe is dead. He died in Baltimore the day before yesterday. This announcement will startle many, but few will be grieved by it. The poet was known, personally or by reputation, in all the country; he had readers in England, and in several of the states of Continental Europe; but he had few or no friends; and the regrets for his death will be suggested principally by the consideration that in him literary art has lost one of its most brilliant but erratic stars."

He wrote that Edgar was a raving lunatic, muttering curses as he stumbled through the streets, drunk and delirious. He went on to say that Edgar was unprincipled, immoral, and repugnant.

Under the guise of benefitting Mrs. Clemm, Griswold convinced Maria to give him power of attorney, enabling him to contract for a new publication of Edgar's writings. In six weeks, he compiled the first two volumes of Edgar's works for publication. He received no payment for the work. Maria Clemm received no monies; the publishers gave her a few free sets for her own use.

During the next six months, several of Edgar's friends tried to defend against Griswold's slanders, but as one noted, "the whole press of the country seemed desirous of giving circulation and authenticity to the slanders." The most lurid stories sold papers.

The collection of Edgar's works sold 1,500 sets a year for many years. For the 1850 edition, Griswold expanded his original obituary to a thirty-five page character assassination of Edgar.

Griswold resorted to fabrication, plagiarism, and forgery. He claimed Edgar was expelled from the University of Virginia, had deserted the army, seduced his foster father's second wife, and been addicted to drugs. He forged many of Edgar's letters and misrepresented others. He wrote that Edgar beat his wife causing her death and had been arrested on multiple occasions. This view of Edgar had the opposite effect on the public than what Griswold wanted. By creating a wicked and scandalous Poe, he ensured that Edgar's work would continue to attract attention.

The revival in stature of Edgar's writing started as early as 1874. In France and England, his popularity soared. The audience finally caught up to the writer who was ahead of his time. Tennyson said he was "the most original genius that America has produced." Thomas Hardy considered him "the first to realize in full the possibility of the English language." Yeats believed he was "the greatest of American poets."

Griswold's twisted biography would stand as the public image of Edgar for almost 100 years until modern biographers revealed a more balanced and honest profile to the public.

For over two hundred years, he has fueled the nightmares of millions. Life kept providing inspiration for his work. He put pen to paper and revealed his morbid fears and unspeakable longings. Yet, he was so much more. He little resembled any writer before him, but almost every writer after resembled him.

Today, long after his critics and contemporaries were forgotten, Edgar Allan Poe has become an industry unto itself. Countless movies, books, articles, artwork, and even toys are produced every year as his stories continue to disturb, delight, and inspire modern generations.

Abot d'après Vierge

THE MURDERS IN THE RUE MORGUE

Act Seven
Chronology

Edgar's aunt, Maria Clemm (Library of Congress)

Chronology of Edgar A. Poe's life and work

1809 Born January 19, Boston to David and Elizabeth Poe

1810 Edgar's father abandons the family (death date uncertain)

1811 Edgar's mother, Elizabeth, dies, December 8 Edgar is taken into the home of merchant John Allan and his wife, Frances (Fanny).

1815–1820 Lives in England with the Allans, attending boarding schools

1825 Courts Elmira Royster, to whom he may have become engaged but never married.

1826 Registers at the University of Virginia on February 14

1827 After Allan refuses to allow Edgar to continue his studies, he leaves home for Boston on April 3. Publishes first collection of poems, *Tamerlane and Other Poems.* Enlists in the U.S. Army under the name Edgar A. Perry.

1828 Rises to the rank of sergeant major in the army before seeking a discharge in order to apply to West Point. Foster mother Fanny Allan dies in February

1829 Second collection of poems, *Al Aaraaf, Tamerlane, and Minor Poems,* is published in Baltimore.

1830 Enters West Point.

1831 Is court-martialed and leaves West Point. Moves to Baltimore and inrto the home of the Clemms, his paternal grandmother, aunt, and cousins. His brother, William Henry, dies August 1. Edgar's third collection of poems, *Poems by Edgar A. Poe. Second Edition,* is published in New York.

1832–1833 Story "MS. Found in a Bottle" wins Baltimore *Saturday Visitor* literary contest.

1834 Foster father, John Allan dies on March 27, leaving Edgar nothing in his will.

1835 Moves to Richmond to become editor of the *Southern Literary Messenger,* in which he publishes stories and reviews that gain him a reputation as a severe critic.

1836 On May 16, marries thirteen year old cousin Virginia Clemm.

1837 Resigns as editor of the *Messenger* and moves to New York with his wife and Aunt, but is unable to find work.

1838 Moves his family to Philadelphia; Publishes his novel *The Narrative of Arthur Gordon Pym* in July.

1839 Ghost writes *The Conchologist's First Book.* Becomes editor of *Burton's Gentleman's Magazine*, writing reviews and stories including "The Fall of the House of Usher" and "William Wilson."

1840 Attempts unsuccessfully to found his own magazine, the *Penn*, and becomes editor of *Graham's Magazine.* Story collection, *Tales of the Grotesque and Arabesque,* published.

1841 Publishes "A Descent into a Maelstrom," "The Murders in the Rue Morgue," and other stories in *Graham's.* Meets Rufus Griswold.

1843 "The Gold-Bug" wins literary contest sponsored by the Philadelphia *Dollar Newspaper. The Prose Romances of Edgar A. Poe* published in Philadelphia. Begins lecturing career.

1844 Returning to New York, Edgar goes to work for the New York *Evening Mirror.* "The Balloon-Hoax" published in New York *Sun.*

1845 "The Raven" published in New York, becoming an immediate success. Edgar becomes editor of the *Broadway Journal* and the in October buys newspaper on borrowed money.

1846 Sues Thomas Dunn English for libel

1847 Virginia Poe dies of tuberculosis on January 30. Edgar publishes the poem "Ulalume" in the *American Review* at the end of the year.

1848 Continues lecturing and publishes a philosophical treatise, *Eureka, A Prose Poem,* in July

1849 Becomes engaged to the widowed Elmira Royster Shelton, his childhood sweetheart. On October 3, found in a delirious condition in Baltimore and dies on October 7. Poems, "The Bells" and "Annabel Lee" are published posthumously.

Act Eight
Selected Poems

The Raven's shadow, Gustave Doré 1884

THE RAVEN

Originally published in January 1845 in several different periodicals, including the New York *Evening Mirror* and the *American Review.*

Once upon a midnight dreary, while I pondered weak and weary,
Over many a quaint and curious volume of forgotten lore,
While I nodded, nearly napping, suddenly there came a tapping,
As of someone gently rapping, rapping at my chamber door.
"Tis some visitor," I muttered, "tapping at my chamber door -
Only this, and nothing more."

Ah, distinctly I remember it was in the bleak December,
And each separate dying ember wrought its ghost upon the floor.
Eagerly I wished the morrow; - vainly I had sought to borrow
From my books surcease of sorrow - sorrow for the lost Lenore -
For the rare and radiant maiden whom the angels name Lenore -
Nameless here for evermore.

And the silken sad uncertain rustling of each purple curtain
Thrilled me - filled me with fantastic terrors never felt before;
So that now, to still the beating of my heart, I stood repeating
"Tis some visitor entreating entrance at my chamber door -
Some late visitor entreating entrance at my chamber door; -
This it is, and nothing more,"

Presently my soul grew stronger; hesitating then no longer,
"Sir," said I, "or Madam, truly your forgiveness I implore;
But the fact is I was napping, and so gently you came rapping,
And so faintly you came tapping, tapping at my chamber door,
That I scarce was sure I heard you" - here I opened wide the door; -
Darkness there, and nothing more.

Deep into that darkness peering, long I stood there wondering,
fearing,
Doubting, dreaming dreams no mortal ever dared to dream before;
But the silence was unbroken, and the darkness gave no token,
And the only word there spoken was the whispered word, "Lenore!"

This I whispered, and an echo murmured back the word, "Lenore!"
Merely this and nothing more.

Back into the chamber turning, all my soul within me burning,
Soon again I heard a tapping somewhat louder than before.
"Surely," said I, "surely that is something at my window lattice;
Let me see then, what thereat is, and this mystery explore -
Let my heart be still a moment and this mystery explore; -
'Tis the wind and nothing more!"

Open here I flung the shutter, when, with many a flirt and flutter,
In there stepped a stately raven of the saintly days of yore.
Not the least obeisance made he; not a minute stopped or stayed he;
But, with mien of lord or lady, perched above my chamber door -
Perched upon a bust of Pallas just above my chamber door -
Perched, and sat, and nothing more.

Then this ebony bird beguiling my sad fancy into smiling,
By the grave and stern decorum of the countenance it wore,
"Though thy crest be shorn and shaven, thou," I said, "art sure no craven.
Ghastly grim and ancient raven wandering from the nightly shore -
Tell me what thy lordly name is on the Night's Plutonian shore!"
Quoth the raven, "Nevermore."'

Much I marvelled this ungainly fowl to hear discourse so plainly,
Though its answer little meaning - little relevancy bore;
For we cannot help agreeing that no living human being
Ever yet was blessed with seeing bird above his chamber door -
Bird or beast above the sculptured bust above his chamber door,
With such name as "Nevermore."

But the raven, sitting lonely on the placid bust, spoke only,
That one word, as if his soul in that one word he did outpour.
Nothing further then he uttered - not a feather then he fluttered -
Till I scarcely more than muttered "Other friends have flown before -
On the morrow he will leave me, as my hopes have flown before."
Then the bird said, "Nevermore."

Startled at the stillness broken by reply so aptly spoken,
"Doubtless,"' said I, "what it utters is its only stock and store,
Caught from some unhappy master whom unmerciful disaster
Followed fast and followed faster till his songs one burden bore -
Till the dirges of his hope that melancholy burden bore
Of 'Never-nevermore'."

But the raven still beguiling all my sad soul into smiling,
Straight I wheeled a cushioned seat in front of bird and bust and door;
Then, upon the velvet sinking, I betook myself to linking
Fancy unto fancy, thinking what this ominous bird of yore -
What this grim, ungainly, ghastly, gaunt, and ominous bird of yore
Meant in croaking "Nevermore."

This I sat engaged in guessing, but no syllable expressing
To the fowl whose fiery eyes now burned into my bosom's core;
This and more I sat divining, with my head at ease reclining
On the cushion's velvet lining that the lamp-light gloated o'er,
But whose velvet violet lining with the lamp-light gloating o'er,
She shall press, ah, nevermore!

Then, methought, the air grew denser, perfumed from an unseen censer
Swung by Seraphim whose foot-falls tinkled on the tufted floor.
"Wretch," I cried, "thy God hath lent thee - by these angels he has sent thee
Respite - respite and nepenthe from thy memories of Lenore!
Quaff, oh quaff this kind nepenthe, and forget this lost Lenore!"
Quoth the raven, "Nevermore."

"Prophet!" said I, "thing of evil! - prophet still, if bird or devil! -
Whether tempter sent, or whether tempest tossed thee here ashore,
Desolate yet all undaunted, on this desert land enchanted -
On this home by horror haunted - tell me truly, I implore -
Is there - is there balm in Gilead? - tell me - tell me, I implore!"
Quoth the raven, "Nevermore."

"Prophet!" said I, "thing of evil! - prophet still, if bird or devil!
By that Heaven that bends above us - by that God we both adore -

Tell this soul with sorrow laden if, within the distant Aidenn,
It shall clasp a sainted maiden whom the angels name Lenore -
Clasp a rare and radiant maiden, whom the angels name Lenore?"
Quoth the raven, "Nevermore."

"Be that word our sign of parting, bird or fiend!" I shrieked upstarting -
"Get thee back into the tempest and the Night's Plutonian shore!
Leave no black plume as a token of that lie thy soul hath spoken!
Leave my loneliness unbroken! - quit the bust above my door!
Take thy beak from out my heart, and take thy form from off my door!"
Quoth the raven, "Nevermore."

And the raven, never flitting, still is sitting, still is sitting
On the pallid bust of Pallas just above my chamber door;
And his eyes have all the seeming of a demon's that is dreaming,
And the lamp-light o'er him streaming throws his shadow on the floor;
And my soul from out that shadow that lies floating on the floor
Shall be lifted - nevermore!

THE BELLS

First published posthumously in *Sartain's Union Magazine,* December 1849

I.

Hear the sledges with the bells--
Silver bells!
What a world of merriment their melody foretells!
How they tinkle, tinkle, tinkle,
In the icy air of night!
While the stars that oversprinkle
All the heavens, seem to twinkle
With a crystalline delight;

Keeping time, time, time,
In a sort of Runic rhyme,
To the tintinnabulation that so musically wells
From the bells, bells, bells, bells,
Bells, bells, bells--
From the jingling and the tinkling of the bells.

II.

Hear the mellow wedding bells
Golden bells!
What a world of happiness their harmony foretells!
Through the balmy air of night
How they ring out their delight!
From the molten-golden notes,
And all in tune,
What a liquid ditty floats
To the turtle-dove that listens, while she gloats
On the moon!
Oh, from out the sounding cells,
What a gush of euphony voluminously wells!
How it swells!
How it dwells
On the Future! how it tells
Of the rapture that impels
To the swinging and the ringing
Of the bells, bells, bells,
Of the bells, bells, bells, bells,
Bells, bells, bells--
To the rhyming and the chiming of the bells!

III.

Hear the loud alarum bells--
Brazen bells!
What tale of terror, now, their turbulency tells!
In the startled ear of night
How they scream out their affright!
Too much horrified to speak,
They can only shriek, shriek,
Out of tune,
In a clamorous appealing to the mercy of the fire,

In a mad expostulation with the deaf and frantic fire,
Leaping higher, higher, higher,
With a desperate desire,
And a resolute endeavor
Now--now to sit or never,
By the side of the pale-faced moon.
Oh, the bells, bells, bells!
What a tale their terror tells
Of Despair!
How they clang, and clash, and roar!
What a horror they outpour
On the bosom of the palpitating air!
Yet the ear, it fully knows,
By the twanging,
And the clanging,
How the danger ebbs and flows ;
Yet, the ear distinctly tells,
In the jangling,
And the wrangling,
How the danger sinks and swells,
By the sinking or the swelling in the anger of the bells--
Of the bells--
Of the bells, bells, bells, bells,
Bells, bells, bells--
In the clamour and the clangour of the bells!

IV.

Hear the tolling of the bells--
Iron bells!
What a world of solemn thought their monody compels!
In the silence of the night,
How we shiver with affright
At the melancholy meaning of their tone!
For every sound that floats
From the rust within their throats
Is a groan.
And the people--ah, the people--
They that dwell up in the steeple,
All alone,
And who, tolling, tolling, tolling,

In that muffled monotone,
Feel a glory in so rolling
On the human heart a stone--
They are neither man nor woman--
They are neither brute nor human--
They are Ghouls:--
And their king it is who tolls ;
And he rolls, rolls, rolls, rolls,
Rolls
A pæan from the bells!
And his merry bosom swells
With the pæan of the bells!
And he dances, and he yells;
Keeping time, time, time,
In a sort of Runic rhyme,
To the pæan of the bells--
Of the bells :
Keeping time, time, time,
In a sort of Runic rhyme,
To the throbbing of the bells--
Of the bells, bells, bells--
To the sobbing of the bells;
Keeping time, time, time,
As he knells, knells, knells,
In a happy Runic rhyme,
To the rolling of the bells--
Of the bells, bells, bells--
To the tolling of the bells,
Of the bells, bells, bells, bells--
Bells, bells, bells--
To the moaning and the groaning of the bells.

ANNABEL LEE

Originally published posthumously in the *Richmond Examiner,* August 1849

It was many and many a year ago,
In a kingdom by the sea,
That a maiden there lived whom you may know
By the name of ANNABEL LEE;
And this maiden she lived with no other thought
Than to love and be loved by me.

I was a child and she was a child,
In this kingdom by the sea;
But we loved with a love that was more than love-
I and my Annabel Lee;
With a love that the winged seraphs of heaven
Coveted her and me.

And this was the reason that, long ago,
In this kingdom by the sea,
A wind blew out of a cloud, chilling
My beautiful Annabel Lee;
So that her highborn kinsman came
And bore her away from me,
To shut her up in a sepulchre
In this kingdom by the sea.

The angels, not half so happy in heaven,
Went envying her and me-
Yes!- that was the reason (as all men know,
In this kingdom by the sea)
That the wind came out of the cloud by night,
Chilling and killing my Annabel Lee.

But our love it was stronger by far than the love
Of those who were older than we-

Of many far wiser than we-
And neither the angels in heaven above,
Nor the demons down under the sea,
Can ever dissever my soul from the soul
Of the beautiful Annabel Lee.

For the moon never beams without bringing me dreams
Of the beautiful Annabel Lee;
And the stars never rise but I feel the bright eyes
Of the beautiful Annabel Lee;
And so, all the night-tide, I lie down by the side
Of my darling- my darling- my life and my bride,
In the sepulchre there by the sea,
In her tomb by the sounding sea.

A DREAM WITHIN A DREAM

A version of this poem originally appeared in
Tamerlane and Other Poems.

Take this kiss upon the brow!
And, in parting from you now,
Thus much let me avow-
You are not wrong, who deem
That my days have been a dream;
Yet if hope has flown away
In a night, or in a day,
In a vision, or in none,
Is it therefore the less gone?
All that we see or seem
Is but a dream within a dream.

I stand amid the roar
Of a surf-tormented shore,
And I hold within my hand
Grains of the golden sand-
How few! yet how they creep

Through my fingers to the deep,
While I weep- while I weep!
O God! can I not grasp
Them with a tighter clasp?
O God! can I not save
One from the pitiless wave?
Is all that we see or seem
But a dream within a dream?

ALONE

Unpublished and untitled in Poe's lifetime, it was written around 1829, and first published in *Scribner's Monthly Magazine,* September 1875.

From childhood's hour I have not been
As others were; I have not seen
As others saw; I could not bring
My passions from a common spring.
From the same source I have not taken
My sorrow; I could not awaken
My heart to joy at the same tone;
And all I loved, I loved alone.
Then- in my childhood, in the dawn
Of a most stormy life- was drawn
From every depth of good and ill
The mystery which binds me still:
From the torrent, or the fountain,
From the red cliff of the mountain,
From the sun that round me rolled
In its autumn tint of gold,
From the lightning in the sky
As it passed me flying by,
From the thunder and the storm,
And the cloud that took the form
(When the rest of Heaven was blue)
Of a demon in my view.

Act Nine
Selected Stories

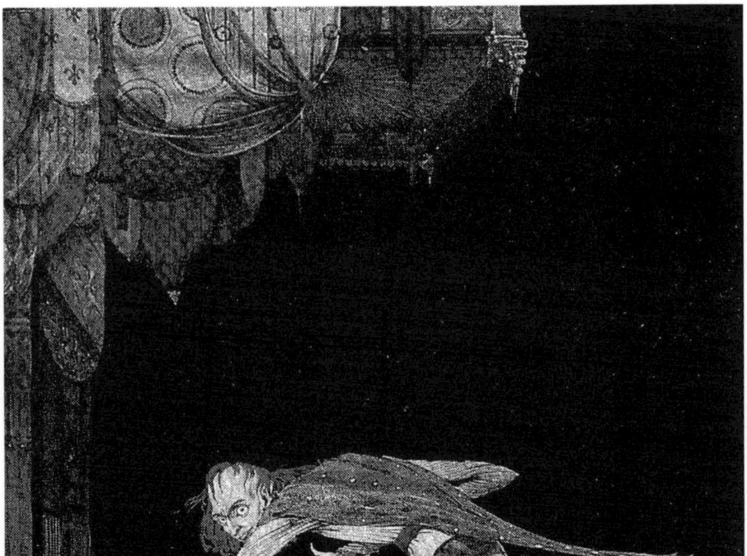

Tell-Tale Heart (Harry Clarke 1923)

THE FACTS IN THE CASE OF M. VALDEMAR

Originally published in both the December 1845, issue of the *Broadway Journal.* Many at the time took it to be a factual account.

OF course, I shall not pretend to consider it any matter for wonder that the extraordinary case of M. Valdemar has excited discussion. It would have been a miracle had it not — especially under the circumstances. Through the desire of all parties concerned to keep the affair from the public, at least for the present, or until we had further opportunities for investigation— through our endeavours to effect this—a garbled or exaggerated account made its way into society, and became the source of many unpleasant misrepresentations; and, very naturally, of a great deal of disbelief.

It is now rendered necessary that I give the facts— as far as I comprehend them myself. They are, succinctly, these :—

My attention, for the last three years, had been repeatedly drawn to the subject of mesmerism; and, about nine months ago, it occurred to me, quite suddenly, that in the series of experiments made hitherto, there had been a very remarkable and most unaccountable omission—no person had as yet been mesmerised in articulo mortis. It remained to be seen, first, whether, in such condition, there existed in the patient any susceptibility to the magnetic influence; secondly, whether, if any existed, it was impaired or increased by the condition; thirdly, to what extent, or for how long a period, the encroachments of Death might be arrested by the process. There were other points to be ascertained, but these most excited my curiosity—the last in especial, from the immensely important character of its consequences.

In looking around me for some subject by whose means I might test these particulars, I was brought to think of my friend, M. Ernest Valdemar, the well-known compiler of the "Bibliotheca Forensics," an author (under the nom de plume of Issachar Marx) of the Polish versions of "Wallenstein" and "Gargantua." M. Valdemar, who has resided principally at Harlem, N. Y., since the year 1839, is (or was) particularly noticeable for the extreme spareness of his person— his lower limbs much resembling those of John Randolph; and, also, for the whiteness of his whiskers, in violent contrast to the blackness of his hair—the latter, in consequence, being very generally mistaken for a wig. His temperament was markedly nervous, and rendered him a good subject for mesmeric experiment. On two or three occasions I had put him to sleep with little difficulty, but was disappointed in other results which his peculiar constitution had naturally led me to anticipate. His will was at no period positively, or thoroughly, under my control; and in regard to clairvoyance, I could accomplish with him nothing to be relied upon. I always attributed my failure at these points to the disordered state of his health. For some months previous to my becoming acquainted with him, his physicians had declared him in a confirmed phthisis. It was his custom, indeed, to speak calmly of his approaching dissolution, as of a matter neither to be avoided nor regretted.

When the ideas to which I have alluded first occurred to me, it was of course very natural that I should think of M. Valdemar. I knew the steady philosophy of the man too well to apprehend any scruples from him; and he had no relatives in America who would be likely to interfere. I spoke to him frankly upon the subject; and, to my surprise, his interest seemed vividly excited. I say to my surprise; for, although he had always yielded his person freely to my experiments, he had never before given me any tokens of sympathy with what I did. His disease was of that character which would admit of exact calculation in respect to the epoch of its termination in death; and it was finally arranged between us that he would send for me about twenty-four hours before the period announced by his physicians as that of his decease.

It is now rather more than seven months since I received, from M.

Valdemar himself, the subjoined note :—

"My Dear P— , You may as well come now. D— and F— are agreed that I cannot hold out beyond to-morrow midnight; and I think they have hit the time very nearly. Valdemar."

I received this note within half-an-hour after it was written, and in fifteen minutes more I was in the dying man's chamber. I had not seen him for ten days, and was appalled by the fearful alteration which the brief interval had wrought in him. His face wore a leaden hue; the eyes were utterly lustreless; and the emaciation was so extreme, that the skin had been broken through by the cheek-bones. His expectoration was excessive. The pulse was barely perceptible. He retained, nevertheless, in a very remarkable manner, both his mental power and a certain degree of physical strength. He spoke with distinctness—took some palliative medicines without aid—and, when I entered the room, was occupied in penciling memoranda in a pocket-book. He was propped up in the bed by pillows. Doctors D— and F— were in attendance. After pressing Valdemar's hand, I took these gentlemen aside, and obtained from them a minute account of the patient's condition. The left lung had been for eighteen months in a semi-osseous or cartilaginous state, and was, of course, entirely useless for all purposes of vitality. The right, in its upper portion, was also partially, if not thoroughly, ossified, while the lower region was merely a mass of purulent tubercles, running one into another. Several extensive perforations existed; and, at one point, permanent adhesion to the ribs had/taken place. These appearances in the right lobe were of comparatively recent date. The ossification had proceeded with very unusual rapidity; no sign of it had been discovered a month before, and the adhesion had only been observed during the three previous days. Independently of the phthisis, the patient was suspected of aneurism of the aorta; but on this point the osseous symptoms rendered an exact diagnosis impossible. It was the opinion of both physicians that M. Valdemar would die about midnight on the morrow (Sunday). It was then seven o'clock on Saturday evening.

On quitting the invalid's bedside to hold conversation with myself, Doctors D and F had bidden him a final farewell. It had not been their intention to return; but, at my request, they agreed to look in upon the patient about ten the next night.

When they had gone, I spoke freely with M. Valdemar on the subject of his approaching dissolution, as well as, more particularly, of the experiment proposed. He still professed himself quite willing and even anxious to have it made, and urged me to commence it at once. A male and a female nurse were in attendance; but I did not feel myself altogether at liberty to engage in a task of this character with no more reliable witnesses than these people, in case of sudden accident, might prove. I therefore postponed operations until about eight the next night, when the arrival of a medical student, with whom I had some acquaintance (Mr. Theodore L—I), relieved me from further embarrassment. It had been my design, originally, to wait for the physicians; but I was induced to proceed, first, by the urgent entreaties of M. Valdemar, and secondly, by my conviction that I had not a moment to lose, as he was evidently sinking fast.

Mr. L —I was Bo kind as to accede to my desire that he would take notes of all that occurred; and it is from his memoranda that what I now have to relate is, for the most part, either condensed or copied verbatim.

It wanted about five minutes of eight when, taking the patient's hand, I begged him to state, as distinctly as he could, to Mr. L—I, whether he (M. Valdemar) was entirely willing that I should make the experiment of mesmerising him in his then condition.

He replied feebly, yet quite audibly, "Yes, I wish to be mesmerized" —adding immediately afterwards, “I fear you have deferred it too long.”

While he spoke thus, I commenced the passes which I had already found most effectual in subduing him. He was evidently influenced with the first lateral stroke of my hand across his forehead; but although I exerted all my powers, no further perceptible effect was induced until some minutes after ten o'clock, when Doctors D— and F— called, according to appointment. I explained to them, in a few words, what I designed, and as they opposed no objection, saying that the patient was already in the death agony, I proceeded without hesitation—exchanging, however, the lateral passes for downward ones, and directing my gaze entirely into the right eye of the sufferer.

By this time his pulse was imperceptible and his breathing was stertorous, and at intervals of half a minute.

This condition was nearly unaltered for a quarter of an hour. At the expiration of this period, however, a natural, although a very deep sigh, escaped the bosom of the dying man, and the stertorous breathing ceased —that is to say, its stertorousness was no longer apparent; the intervals were undiminished. The patient's extremities were of an icy coldness.

At five minutes before eleven I perceived unequivocal signs of the mesmeric influence. The glassy roll of the eye was changed for that expression of uneasy inward examination which is never seen except in cases' of sleep-waking, and which it is quite impossible to mistake. With a few rapid lateral passes I made the lids quiver, as in incipient sleep, and with a few more I closed them altogether. I was not satisfied, however, with this, but continued the manipulations vigorously, and with the fullest exertion of the will, until I had completely stiffened the limbs of the slumberer, after placing them in a seemingly easy position. The legs were at full length; the arms were nearly so, and reposed on the bed at a moderate distance from the loins. The head was very slightly elevated.

When I had accomplished this, it was fully midnight, and I requested the gentlemen present to examine M. Valdemar's condition. After a few experiments, they admitted him to be in an unusually perfect state of mesmeric trance. The curiosity of both the physicians was greatly excited. Dr. D— resolved at once to remain with the patient all night, while Dr. F— took leave with a promise to return at daybreak. Mr. L— I and the nurses remained.

We left M. Valdemar entirely undisturbed until about three o'clock in the morning, when I approached him, and found him in precisely the same condition as when Dr. F— went away—that is to say, he lay in the same position. The pulse was imperceptible; the breathing was gentle (scarcely noticeable, unless through the application of a mirror to the lips); the eyes were closed naturally; and the limbs were as rigid and as cold as marble. Still, the general appearance was certainly not that of death.

As I approached M. Valdemar I made a kind of half effort to influence his right arm into pursuit of my own, as I passed the latter gently to and fro above his person. In such experiments with this patient I had never perfectly succeeded before, and assuredly I had little thought of succeeding now; but to my astonishment, his arm very readily, although feebly, followed every direction I assigned it with mine. I determined to hazard a few words of conversation.

"M. Valdemar," I said, "are you asleep?" He made no answer, but I perceived a tremor about the lips, and was thus induced to repeat the question, again and again. At its third repetition, his whole frame was agitated by a very slight shivering ; the eyelids unclosed themselves so far as to display a white line of a ball; the lips moved sluggishly, and from between them, in a barely audible whisper, issued the words—

"Yes; asleep now. Do not wake me !—let me die so!"

I here felt the limbs and found them as rigid as ever. The right arm, as before, obeyed the direction of my hand. I questioned the sleep-waker again—

"Do you still feel pain in the breast, M. Valdemar?"

The answer now was immediate, but even less audible than before—

"No pain—I am dying."

I did not think it advisable to disturb him further just then, and nothing more was said or done until the arrival of Dr. F— , who came a little before sunrise, and expressed unbounded astonishment at finding the patient still alive. After feeling the pulse and applying a mirror to the lips, he requested me to speak to the sleep-waker again. I did so, saying—

"M. Valdemar, do you still sleep?"

As before, some minutes elapsed ere a reply was made; and during the interval the dying man seemed to be collecting his energies to speak. At my fourth repetition of the question, he said very faintly, almost inaudibly—

"Yes; still asleep—dying."

It was now the opinion, or rather the wish, of the physicians, that M. Valdemar should be suffered to remain undisturbed in his present apparently tranquil condition, until death should supervene—and this, it was generally agreed, must now take place within a few minutes. I concluded, however, to speak to him once more, and merely repeated my previous question.

While I spoke, there came a marked change over the countenance of the sleep-waker. The eyes rolled themselves slowly open, the pupils disappearing upwardly; the skin generally assumed a cadaverous hue, resembling not so much parchment as white paper; and the circular hectic spots which, hitherto, had been strongly defined in the centre of each cheek, went out at once. I use this expression, because the suddenness of their departure put me in mind of nothing so much as the extinguishment of a candle by a puff of the breath. The upper lip, at the same time, writhed itself away from the teeth, which it had previously covered completely; while the lower jaw fell with an audible jerk, leaving the mouth widely extended, and disclosing in full view the swollen and blackened tongue. I presume that no member of the party then present had been unaccustomed to death-bed horrors; but so hideous beyond conception was the appearance of M. Valdemar at this moment, that there was a general shrinking back from the region of the bed.

I now feel that I have reached a point of this narrative at which every reader will be startled into positive disbelief. It is my business, however simply to proceed.

There was no longer the faintest sign of vitality in M. Valdemar; and concluding him to be dead, we were consigning him to the charge of the nurses, when a strong vibratory motion was observable in the tongue. This continued for perhaps a minute. At the expiration of this period, there issued from the distended and motionless jaws a voice—such as it would be madness in me to attempt describing. There are, indeed, two or three epithets which might be considered as applicable to it in part; I might say, for example, that the sound was harsh, and broken, and hollow; but the hideous whole is indescribable, for the simple reason that no similar sounds have ever jarred upon the ear of humanity. There were two particulars, nevertheless, which I thought then, and still think, might fairly be stated as characteristic of the intonation — as well adapted to convey some idea of its unearthly peculiarity. In the first place, the voice seemed to reach our ears—at least mine—from a vast distance, or from some deep cavern within the earth. In the second place, it impressed me (I fear, indeed, that it will be impossible to make myself comprehended) as gelatinous or glutinous matters impress the sense of touch.

I have spoken both of "sound" and of "voice." I mean to say that the sound was one of distinct—of even wonderfully, thrillingly distinct—syllabification. M. Valdemar spoke—obviously in reply to the question I had propounded to him a few minutes before. I had asked him, it will be remembered, if he still slept. He now said—

"Yes—no—I have been sleeping—and now—now —I am dead."

No person present even affected to deny, or attempted to repress, the unutterable, shuddering horror which these few words, thus uttered, were so well calculated to convey. Mr. L— I (the student) swooned. The nurses immediately left the chamber, and could not be induced to return. My own impressions I would not pretend to render intelligible, to the reader. For nearly an hour, we busied ourselves, silently— without the utterance of a word—in endeavours to revive Mr. L— I. When he came to himself, we addressed ourselves again to an investigation of M. Valdemar's condition.

It remained in all respects as I have last described it, with the exception that the mirror no longer afforded evidence of respiration. An attempt to draw blood from the arm failed. I should mention, too, that this limb was no further subject to my will. I endeavoured in vain to make it follow the direction of my hand. The only real indication, indeed, of the mesmeric influence was now found in the vibratory movement of the tongue, whenever I addressed M. Valdemar a question. He seemed to be making an effort to reply, but had no longer sufficient volition. To queries put to him by any other person than myself he seemed utterly insensible — although I endeavoured to place each member of the company in mesmeric rapport with him. I believe that I have now related all that is necessary to an understanding of the sleep- waiter's state at this epoch. Other nurses were procured; and at ten o'clock I left the house in company with the two physicians and Mr. L—I.

In the afternoon we all called again to see the patient. His condition remained precisely the same. We had now some discussion as to the propriety and feasibility of awakening him; but we had little difficulty in agreeing that no good purpose would be served by so doing. It was evident that, so far, death (or what is usually termed death) had been arrested by the mesmeric process. It seemed clear to us all that to awaken M. Valdemar would be merely to insure his instant, or at least his speedy dissolution.

From this period until the close of last week—an interval of nearly seven months—we continued to make daily calls at M. Valdemar's house, accompanied, now and then, by medical and other friends. All this time the sleep-waker remained exactly as I have last described him. The nurses' attentions were continual.

It was on Friday last that we finally resolved to make the experiment of awakening, or attempting to awaken him; and it is the (perhaps) unfortunate result of this latter experiment which has given rise to so much discussion in private circles—to so much of what I cannot help thinking unwarranted popular feeling.

For the purpose of relieving M. Valdemar from the mesmeric trance, I made use of the customary passes. These for a time were unsuccessful. The first indication of revival was afforded by a partial descent of the iris. It was observed, as especially remarkable, that this lowering of the pupil was accompanied by the profuse outflowing of a yellowish ichor (from beneath the lids) of a pungent and highly offensive odour.

It was now suggested that I should attempt to influence the patient's arm as heretofore. I made the attempt and failed. Dr. F— then intimated a desire to have me put a question. I did so, as follows—

"M. Valdemar, can you explain to us what are your feelings or wishes now ?"

There was an instant return of the hectic circles on the cheeks ; the tongue quivered, or rather rolled violently in the mouth (although the jaws and lips remained rigid as before); and at length the same hideous voice which I have already described, broke forth—

"For God's sake !—quick !—quick—put me to sleep —or quick !—waken me !—quick !—I say to you that I am dead !"

I was thoroughly unnerved, and for an instant remained undecided what to do. At first I made an endeavour to re-compose the patient; but, failing in this through total abeyance of the will, I retraced my steps, and as earnestly struggled to awaken him. In this attempt I soon saw that I should be successful—or at least I soon fancied that my success would be complete—and I am sure that all in the room were prepared to see the patient awaken.

For what really occurred, however, it is quite impossible that any human being could have been prepared.

As I rapidly made the mesmeric passes, amid ejaculations of "Dead! dead !" absolutely bursting from the tongue and not from the lips of the sufferer, his whole frame at once—within the space of a single minute, or even less, shrunk—crumbled—absolutely rotted away beneath my hands. Upon the bed, before that whole company, there lay a nearly liquid mass of loathsome —of detestable putrescence.

THE TELL-TALE HEART

Originally published in January 1843 in *The Pioneer* magazine; Poe revised the tale and published it again in the *Broadway Journal* in 1845. (*This is also the story that turned me on to Poe —William.*)

TRUE!—nervous—very, very dreadfully nervous I had been and am; but why will you say that I am mad? The disease had sharpened my senses—not destroyed —not dulled them. Above all was the sense of hearing acute. I heard all things in the heaven and in the earth. I heard many things in hell. How, then, am I mad? Hearken! and observe how healthily—how calmly I can tell you the whole story.

It is impossible to say how first the idea entered my brain; but once conceived, it haunted me day and night. Object there was none. Passion there was none. I loved the old man. He had never wronged me. He had never given me insult. For his gold I had no desire. I think it was his eye! yes, it was this! One of his eyes resembled that of a vulture—a pale blue eye, with a film over it. Whenever it fell upon me, my blood ran cold; and so by degrees—very gradually—I made up my mind to take the life of the old man, and thus rid myself of the eye forever.

Now this is the point. You fancy me mad. Madmen know nothing. But you should have seen me. You should have seen how wisely I proceeded—with what caution—with what foresight—with what dissimulation I went to work! I was never kinder to the old man than during the whole week before I killed him. And every night, about midnight, I turned the latch of his door and opened it—oh, so gently! And then, when I had made an opening sufficient for my head, I put in it dark lantern, all closed, closed, so that no light shone out, and then I thrust in my head. Oh, you would have laughed to see how cunningly I thrust it in! I moved it slowly—very, very slowly, so that I might not disturb the old man's sleep. It took me an hour to place my whole head within the opening so far that I could see him as he lay upon his bed. Ha!—would a madman have been so wise as this? And then, when my head was well in the room, I undid the lantern, cautiously — oh, so cautiously — cautiously (for the hinges creaked) I undid it just so much that a single thin ray fell upon the vulture eye. And this I did for seven long nights—every night just at midnight—but I found the eye always closed; and so it was impossible to do the work; for it was not the old man who vexed me, but his Evil Eye. And every morning, when the day broke, I went boldly into the chamber, and spoke courageously to him, calling him by name in a hearty tone, and inquiring how he had passed the night. So you see he would have been a very profound old man, indeed, to suspect that every night, just at twelve, I looked in upon him while he slept.

Upon the eighth night I was more than usually cautious in opening the door. A watch's minute hand moves more quickly than did mine. Never before that night had I felt the extent of my own powers—of my sagacity. I could scarcely contain my feelings of triumph. To think that there I was, opening the door, little by little, and he not even to dream of my secret deeds or thoughts. I fairly chuckled at the idea; and perhaps he heard me—for he moved on the bed suddenly, as if startled. Now you may think that I drew back—but no. His room was as black as pitch with the thick darkness (for the shutters were close fastened, through fear of robbers), and so I knew that he could not see the opening of the door, and I kept pushing it on steadily, steadily.

I had my head in, and was about to open the lantern, when my thumb slipped upon the tin fastening, and the old man sprang up in the bed, crying out, "Who's there?"

I kept quite still and said nothing. For a whole hour I did not move a muscle, and in the meantime I did not hear him lie down. He was still sitting up in the bed, listening—just as I have done, night after night, hearkening to the death-watches in the wall.

Presently I heard a groan, and I knew it was the groan of mortal terror. It was not a groan of pain or of grief—oh, no!—it was the low stifled sound that arises from the bottom of the soul when overcharged with awe. I knew the sound well. Many a night, just at midnight, when all the world slept, it has welled up from my own bosom, deepening, with its dreadful echo, the terrors that distracted me. I say I knew it well. I knew what the old man felt, and pitied him, although I chuckled at heart. I knew that he had been lying awake ever since the first slight noise, when he had turned in the bed. His fears had been ever since growing upon him. He had been trying to fancy them causeless, but could not. He had been saying to himself, "It is nothing but the wind in the chimney—it is only a mouse crossing the floor," or, "It is merely a cricket which has made a single chirp." Yes, he had been trying to comfort himself with these suppositions; but he had found all in vain. All in vain; because Death, in approaching him, had stalked with his black shadow before him, and enveloped the victim. And it was the mournful influence of the unperceived shadow that caused him to feel—although he neither saw nor heard—to feel the presence of my head within the room.

When I had waited a long time, very patiently, without hearing him lie down, I resolved to open a little—a very, very little crevice in the lantern. So I opened it—you cannot imagine how stealthily; stealthily—until, at length, a single dim ray, like the thread of the spider, shot from out the crevice and fell upon the vulture eye.

It was open—wide, wide open—and I grew furious as I gazed upon it. I saw it with perfect distinctness—all a dull blue, with a hideous veil over it that chilled the very marrow in my bones; but I could see nothing else of the old man's face or person, for I had directed the ray, as if by instinct, precisely upon the damned spot .

And now have I not told you that what you mistake for madness is but over-acuteness of the senses?—now, I say, there came to my ears a low, dull, quick sound, such as a watch makes when enveloped in cotton.

I knew that sound well, too. It was the beating of the old man's heart. It increased my fury, as the beating of a drum stimulates the soldier into courage.

But even yet I refrained and kept still I scarcely breathed. I held the lantern motionless. I tried how steadily I could maintain the ray upon the eye. Meantime the hellish tattoo of the heart increased. It grew quicker and quicker, and louder and louder every instant. The old man's terror must have been extreme 1 It grew louder, I say, louder every moment!—do you mark me well? I have told you that I am nervous: so I am. And now, at the dead hour of the night, amid the dreadful silence of that old house, so strange a noise as this excited me to uncontrollable terror. Yet, for some minutes longer, I refrained and stood still. But the beating grew louder, louder! I thought the heart must burst. And now a new anxiety seized me—the sound would be heard by a neighbour. The old man's hour had come! With a loud yell I threw open the lantern and leaped into the room. He shrieked once—once only. In an instant I dragged him to the floor, and pulled the heavy bed over him. I then smiled gaily, to find the deed so far done. But, for many minutes, the heart beat on with a muffled sound. This, however, did not vex me; it would not be heard through the wall. At length it ceased. The old man was dead. I removed the bed and examined the corpse. Yes, he was stone, stone dead. I placed my hand upon the heart and held it there many minutes. There was no pulsation. He was stone dead. His eye would trouble me no more.

If still you think me mad, you will think so no longer when I describe the wise precautions I took for the concealment of the body. The night waned, and I worked hastily, but in silence. First of all I dismembered the corpse. I cut off the head and the arms and the legs.

I then took up three planks from the flooring of the chamber and deposited all between the scantlings. I then replaced the boards so cleverly, so cunningly, that no human eye—not even his—could have detected anything wrong. There was nothing to wash out—no stain of any kind—no blood-spot whatever. I had been too wary for that. A tub had caught all—ha! ha!

When I had made an end of these labours, it was four o'clock—still dark as midnight. As the bell sounded the hour, there came by knocking at the street door. I went down to open it with a light heart-- for what had I now to fear? There entered three men, who introduced themselves, with perfect suavity, as officers of the police. A shriek had been heard by a neighbour during the night; suspicion of foul play had been aroused; information had been lodged at the police office, and they (the officers) had been deputed to search the premises.

I smiled—for what had I to fear? I bade the gentlemen welcome. The shriek, I said, was my own in a dream. The old man, I mentioned, was absent in the country. I took my visitors all over the house. I bade them search—search well. I led them, at length, to his chamber. I showed them his treasures, secure, undisturbed. In the enthusiasm of my confidence, I brought chairs into the room, and desired them here to rest from their fatigues, while I myself, in the wild audacity of my perfect triumph, placed my own seat upon the very spot—beneath which reposed the corpse of the victim.

The officers were satisfied. My manner had convinced them. I was singularly at ease. They sat, and while I answered cheerily, they chatted of familiar things. But, ere long, I felt myself getting pale and wished them gone. My head ached, and I fancied a ringing in my ears; but still they sat and still chatted. The ringing became more distinct—it continued and became more distinct. I talked more freely to get rid of the feeling; but it continued and gained definitiveness—until, at length, I found that the noise was not within my ears.

No doubt I now grew very pale; but I talked more fluently, and with a heightened voice. Yet the sound increased—and what could I do? It was a low, dull, quick sound—much such a sound as a watch makes when enveloped in cotton. I gasped for breath—and yet the officers heard it not. I talked more quickly—more vehemently; but the noise steadily increased. I arose and argued about trifles, in a high key and with violent gesticulations; but the noise steadily increased. Why would they not be gone? I paced the floor to and fro with heavy strides, as if excited to fury by the observations of the men—but the noise steadily increased. O God! what could I do? I foamed—I raved—I swore! I swung the chair upon which I had been sitting, and grated it upon the boards, but the noise arose over all and continually increased. It grew louder—louder—louder! And still the men chatted pleasantly, and smiled. Was it possible they heard not? Almighty God! —no, no! They heard!—they suspected! —they knew I—they were making a mockery of my horror!—this I thought, and this I think. But anything was better than this agony! Anything was more tolerable than this derision! I could bear those hypocritical smiles no longer! I felt that I must scream or die!—and now— again I hark! louder! louder! louder! *Louder!*

"Villains" I shrieked, “dissemble no more! I admit the deed!—tear up the planks!—here, here!— it is the beating of his hideous heart!”

THE CASK OF AMONTILLADO

This story was first published in *Godey's Lady's Book,* November 1846

THE thousand injuries of Fortunato I had borne as I best could; but when he ventured upon insult, I vowed revenge. You, who so well know the nature of my soul, will not suppose, however, that I gave utterance to a threat. At length I would be avenged; this was a point definitely settled — but the very definitiveness with which it was resolved, precluded the idea of risk. I must not only punish, but punish with impunity. A wrong is unredressed when retribution overtakes its redresser. It is equally unredressed when the avenger fails to make himself felt as such to him who has done the wrong.

It must be understood, that neither by word nor deed had I given Fortunato cause to doubt my goodwill. I continued, as was my wont, to smile in his face, and he did not perceive that my smile now was at the thought of his immolation.

He had a weak point—this Fortunato—although in other regards he was a man to be respected and even feared. He prided himself on his connoisseurship in wine. Few Italians have the true virtuoso spirit . For the most part their enthusiasm is adapted to suit the time and opportunity—to practise imposture upon the British and Austrian millionaires. In painting and gemmary Fortunato, like his countrymen, was a quack —but in the matter of old wines he was sincere. In this respect I did not differ from him materially: I was skillful in the Italian vintages myself, and bought largely whenever I could.

It was about dusk, one evening during the supreme madness of the Carnival season, that I encountered my friend. He accosted me with excessive warmth, for he had been drinking much. The man wore motley. He had on two tight-fitting parti-striped dress, and his head was surmounted by the conical cap and bells. I was so pleased to see him, that I thought I should never have done wringing his hand.

I said to him, "My dear Fortunato, you are luckily met. How remarkably well you are looking to-day I But I have received a pipe of what passes for Amontillado, and I have my doubts."

"How?" said he; "Amontillado? A pipe? Impossible! And in the middle of the carnival!"

"I have my doubts," I replied; "and I was silly enough to pay the full Amontillado price without consulting you in the matter. You were not to be found, and I was fearful of losing a bargain."

"Amontillado!"

"I have my doubts."

"Amontillado!"

"And I must satisfy them."

"Amontillado!"

"As you are engaged, I am on my way to Luchesi. If anyone has a critical turn, it is he. He will tell me."

"Luchesi cannot tell Amontillado from Sherry."

"And yet some fools will have it that his taste is it match for your own."

"Come, let us go."

"Whither?"

"To your vaults."

"My friend, no; I will not impose upon your good-nature. I perceive you have an engagement. Luchesi"

"I have no engagement; come."

"My friend, no. It is not the engagement, but the severe cold with which I perceive you are afflicted. The vaults are insufferably damp. They are encrusted with nitre."

"Let us go nevertheless. The cold is merely nothing. Amontillado! You have been imposed upon. And as for Luchesi—he cannot distinguish Sherry from Amontillado."

Thus speaking, Fortunato possessed himself of my arm. Putting on a mask of black silk, and drawing a roquelaire closely about my person, I suffered him to hurry me to my palazzo.

There were no attendants at home; they had absconded to make merry in honour of the time. I had told them that I should not return until the morning, and had given them explicit orders not to stir from the house. These orders were sufficient, I well knew, to ensure their immediate disappearance, one and all, as soon as my back was turned.

I took from their sconces two flambeaux, and giving one to Fortunato, bowed him through several suites of rooms to the archway that led into the vaults. I passed down a long and winding staircase, requesting him to be cautious as he followed. We came at length to the foot of the descent, and stood together on the damp ground of the catacombs of the Montresors.

The gait of my friend was unsteady, and the bells upon his cap jingled as he strode.

"The pipe," said he.

"It is farther on," said I; "but observe the white webwork which gleams from these cavern walls."

He turned towards me, and looked into my eyes with two filmy orbs that distilled the rheum of intoxication.

"Nitre?" he asked, at length.

"Nitre," I replied. "How long have you had that cough?"

"Ugh! ugh! ugh !—ugh! ugh! ugh!—ugh I ugh! ugh!—ugh! ugh! ugh!:—ugh! ugh! ugh!"

My poor friend found it impossible to reply for many minutes.

"It is nothing," he said, at last.

"Come," I said, with decision, "we will go back; your health is precious. You are rich, respected, admired, beloved; you are happy, as once I was. You are a man to be missed. For me it is no matter. We will go back; you will be ill, and I cannot be responsible. Besides, there is

Luchesi"

"Enough," he said, "the cough is a mere nothing; it will not kill me. I shall not die of a cough."

"True—true," I replied; "and, indeed, I had no intention of alarming you unnecessarily—but you should use all proper caution. A draught of this Medoc will defend us from the damps."

Here I knocked off the neck of a bottle which I drew from a long row of its fellows that lay upon the mould.

"Drink," I said, presenting him the wine.

He raised it to his lips with a leer. He paused and nodded to me familiarly, while his bells jingled.

"I drink," he said, "to the buried that repose around us."

"And I to your long life."

He again took my arm, and we proceeded.

"These vaults," he said, "are extensive."

"The Montresors," I replied, "were a great and numerous family."

"I forget your arms."

"A huge human foot d'or, in a field azure; the foot crushes a serpent rampant whose fangs are embedded in the heel."

"And the motto?"

"Nemo me impune lacessit."

"Good!" he said.

The wine sparkled in his eyes and the bells jingled. My own fancy grew warm with the Medoc. We had passed through walls of piled bones, with casks and puncheons intermingling, into the inmost recesses of the catacombs. I paused again, and this time I made bold to seize Fortunate by an arm above the elbow.

"The nitre!" I said; "see, it increases. It hangs like moss upon the vaults. We are below the river's bed. The drops of moisture trickle among the bones. Come, we will go back ere it is too late. Your cough—"

"It is nothing," he said; "let us go on. But first, another draught of the Medoc."

I broke and reached him a flagon of De Grave. He emptied it at a breath. His eyes flashed with a fierce light. He laughed and threw the bottle upwards with a gesticulation I did not understand.

I looked at him in surprise. He repeated the movement—a grotesque one.

"You do not comprehend?" he said.

"Not I," I replied.

"Then you are not of the brotherhood."

"How?"

"You are not of the masons."

"Yes, yes," I said; "yes, yes."

"You? Impossible! A mason?"

"A mason," I replied.

"A sign," he said.

"It is this," I answered, producing a trowel from beneath the folds of my roquelaire.

"You jest," he exclaimed, recoiling a few paces. "But let us proceed to the Amontillado."

"Be it so," I said, replacing the tool beneath the cloak, and again offering him my arm. He leaned upon it heavily. We continued our route in search of the Amontillado. We passed through a range of low arches, descended, passed on, and descending again, arrived at a deep crypt, in which the foulness of the air caused our flambeaux rather to glow than flame.

At the most remote end of the crypt there appeared another less spacious. Its walls had been lined with human remains, piled to the vault overhead, in the fashion of the great catacombs of Paris. Three sides of this interior crypt were still ornamented in this manner. From the fourth the bones had been thrown down, and lay promiscuously upon the earth, forming at one point a mound of some size. Within the wall thus exposed by the displacing of the bones, we perceived a still interior recess, in depth about four feet, in width three, in height six or seven. It seemed to have been constructed for no especial use within itself, but formed merely the interval between two of the colossal supports of the roof of the catacombs, and was backed by one of their circumscribing walls of solid granite.

It was in vain that Fortunate, uplifting his dull torch, endeavoured to pry into the depth of the recess.

Its' termination the feeble light did not enable us to see.

"Proceed," I said; "herein is the Amontillado. As for Luchesi—"

"He is an ignoramus," interrupted my friend, as he stepped unsteadily forward, while I followed immediately at his heels. In an instant he had reached the extremity of the niche, and finding his progress arrested by the rock, stood stupidly bewildered. A moment more and I had fettered him to the granite. In its surface were two iron staples, distant from each other about two feet, horizontally. From one of these depended a short chain, from the other a padlock. Throwing the links about his waist, it was but the work of a few seconds to secure it. He was too much astounded to resist. Withdrawing the key, I stepped back from the recess.

"Pass your hand," I said, "over the wall; you cannot help feeling the nitre. Indeed it is very damp. Once more let me implore you to return. No? Then I must positively leave you. But I must first render you all the little attentions in my power."

"The Amontillado!" ejaculated my friend, not yet recovered from his astonishment.

"True," I replied, "the Amontillado."

As I said these words I busied myself among the pile of bones of which I have before spoken. Throwing them aside, I soon uncovered a quantity of building stone and mortar. With these materials, and with the aid of my trowel, I began vigorously to wall up the entrance of the niche.

I had scarcely laid the first tier of the masonry when I discovered that the intoxication of Fortunato had in a great measure worn off. The earliest indication I had of this was a low moaning cry from the depth of the recess. It was not the cry of a drunken man. There was then a long and obstinate silence. I laid the second tier, and the third, and the fourth; and then I heard the furious vibrations of the chain. The noise lasted for several minutes, during which, that I might hearken to it with the more satisfaction, I ceased my labours and sat down upon the bones. When at last the clanking subsided, I resumed the trowel, and finished without interruption the fifth, the sixth, and tho seventh tier. The wall was now nearly upon a level with my breast. I again paused, and holding the flambeaux over the masou-work, threw a few feeble rays upon the figure within.

A succession of loud and shrill screams, bursting suddenly from the throat of the chained form, seemed to thrust me violently back. For a brief moment I hesitated—I trembled. Unsheathing my rapier, I began to grope with it about the recess; but the thought of an instant reassured me. I placed my hand upon the solid fabric of the catacombs, and felt satisfied. I approached the wall. I replied to the yells of him who clamoured. I re-echoed—I aided—I surpassed them in volume and in strength. I did this, and the clamourer grew still.

It was now midnight, and my task was drawing to a close, I had completed the eighth, the ninth, and the tenth tier. I had finished a portion of the last and the eleventh; there remained but a single stone to be fitted and plastered in. I struggled with its weight; I placed it partially in its destined position. But now there came from out the niche a low laugh that erected the hairs upon my head. It was succeeded by a sad voice, which I had difficulty in recognising as that of the noble Fortunato. The voice said—

"Ha! ha! ha!—he! he!—a very good joke indeed —an excellent jest. We will have many a rich laugh about it at the palazzo—he! he! he!—over our wine —he! he! he!"

"The Amontillado!" I said.

"He! he! he!—he! he! he!—yes, the Amontillado. But is it not getting late? Will not they be awaiting us at the palazzo, the Lady Fortunato and the rest? Let us be gone."

"Yes," I said, "let us be gone."

"For the love of God, Montreiort"

"Yes," I said, "for the love of God!"

But to these words I hearkened in vain for a reply. I grew impatient. I called aloud—

"Fortunato!"

No answer. I called again—

"Fortunato!"

No answer still. I thrust a torch through the remaining aperture and let it fall within. There came forth in return only a jingling of the bells. My heart grew sick—on account of the dampness of the catacombs. I hastened to make an end of my labour. I forced the last stone into its position; I plastered it up. Against the new masonry I re-erected the old rampart of bones. For the half of it century no mortal has disturbed them. In pace requiescat!

Gustave Doré “Wandering the night shore” 1884

Bibliography

Ackroyd, Peter. *Poe: A Life Cut Short,* (New York, 2008)

Bloom, Harold (Editor). *Edgar Allan Poe, Modern Critical Views,* (New York, 1985)

Hutchisson, James M. *Poe,* (Jackson, MS. 2005)

Johnson, Cynthia Brantley (Editor). *Great Tales and Poems of Edgar Allan Poe,* (New York, 2007)

Meyers, Jeffrey. *Edgar Allan Poe: His Life and Legacy,* (New York, 1992)

Haining, Peter. *The Edgar Allan Poe Scrapbook: Articles, essays, letters, anecdotes, illustrations, photographs, and memorabilia about the legendary American genius,* (New York, 1978)

Quinn, Patrick F. (Editor). *Poe: Poetry, Tales, and Selected Essays* (Library of America College Editions, New York, 1996)

Silverman, Kenneth. *Edgar A. Poe: Mournful and Never-ending Remembrance,* (New York, 1991)

Stashower, Daniel. *The Beautiful Cigar Girl: Mary Rogers, Edgar Allan Poe, and the Invention of Murder,* (New York 2006)

Walker, I.M. (Editor). *Edgar Allan Poe: The Critical Heritage,* (London, 1986)

Walsh, John Evangelist. *Midnight Dreary: The Mysterious Death of Edgar Allan Poe,* (New Brunswick, 1998)

Additional books by William Pack

The Essential Houdini

The Essential P.T. Barnum

The Discovery of Magic

The Essential Great Chicago Fire

Available through williampack.com

"If you want to watch a group of adults mesmerized at an event, invite William. Three weeks later, those who attended still comment on the program. William captivated us with his stories. He brings energy, wit, and fascinating props and illustrations to a terrific program that will stay with you and your patrons. He engages the audience at every step of the program, entertains and educates with a twinkle in his eye."
-Elke Saylor Muskego Library, WI

William is available for magic performances or educational performance lectures custom suited for your event. For more information, please visit williampack.com

**To contact William,
email: bill@williampack.com**

Made in the
USA
Columbia, SC

78939610R00076